COPENHAGEN
& THE BEST OF
DENMARK

ALIVE!

Norman P.T. Renouf

HUNTER

Hunter Publishing, Inc.
130 Campus Drive
Edison, NJ 08818-7816
☎ 732-225-1900 / 800-255-0343 / Fax 732-417-1744
Web site: www.hunterpublishing.com
E-mail: comments@hunterpublishing.com

IN CANADA
Ulysses Travel Publications
4176 Saint-Denis, Montréal, Québec
Canada H2W 2M5
☎ 514-843-9882 ext. 2232 / Fax 514-843-9448

IN THE UK
Windsor Books International
The Boundary, Wheatley Road
Garsington, Oxford OX44 9EJ England
☎ 01865-361122 / Fax 01865-361133

ISBN 1-58843-355-2
© 2003 Hunter Publishing, Inc.

Front Cover: Baroque Garden, Hillerød, *Klaus Bentzen*
Back Cover: Queen Louise's Bridge, Copenhagen, *Jreneusz Cyranek*
Photos Courtesy of Danish Tourist Board
Maps by Toni Wheeler, © 2003 Hunter Publishing, Inc.
Index by Nancy Wolff

4 3 2 1

Contents

Ribe

Index

Maps

About the Author

Norman P.T. Renouf is a prolific writer. His previous books for Hunter Publishing are *Romantic Weekends: The Carolinas & The Georgia Coast*; *Romantic Weekends: Virginia, Maryland & Washington DC* (both co-authored with his wife, Kathy Renouf); and *Adventure Guide to The Georgia & Carolina Coasts*, co-authored with Blair Howard.

About the Alive Guides

Reliable, detailed and personally researched by knowledgeable authors, the *Alive!* series was founded by Harriet and Arnold Greenberg. This accomplished travel-writing team established the renowned bookstore, **The Complete Traveller**, at 199 Madison Avenue in New York City.

We Love to Get Mail

This book has been carefully researched to bring you current, accurate information. But no place is unchanging. We welcome your comments for future editions. Please write us at *Alive Guides*, c/o Hunter Publishing, 130 Campus Drive, Edison, NJ 08818, or send an e-mail to comments@hunterpublishing.com. Due to the volume of mail we receive, we regret that we cannot personally reply to each letter or message, but your comments will be greatly appreciated.

Introduction

Denmark is made up of three regions. Much of the country consists of a group of islands of varying sizes. The large island closest to Sweden is called **Zealand** (*Sjælland*), and is the location of Copenhagen, Helsingør, Hillerød and Roskilde. **Funen** (*Fyn*), where Odense is located, is a smaller island west of Zealand. The largest portion of the country is **Jutland** (*Jylland*), a peninsula connected to Germany and the location of Århus and Ribe.

A Brief History

The Rise of a Kingdom

Initially, some 1,000 years ago, Copenhagen – **København** in Danish – was but a small trading center, specializing in the plentiful supply of local herring; it was also a base for ferry services to **Scania** on the other side of the Øresund (the sound between Denmark and Sweden). Copenhagen's – and Denmark's – fortunes rose dramatically during the 12th and 13th centuries (due in part to the immense demand in mainly Catholic Europe for salted herring during Lent), and the era saw many churches and abbeys founded. Copenhagen's oldest seal dates from 1296, and many of its features are incorporated into the city's present coat of arms. Copenhagen's strategic location – near the approach to the **Baltic Sea** and the North German trading towns of the **Hanseatic League** – brought prosperity, but it also brought problems as a result of repeated attacks. During this period, too, the Danish kings tried to regain control from the bishops. In 1416, **King Erik of Pomerania** finally gained control of the town. Prosperity continued apace and Co-

Denmark & Southern Sweden

Skagerrak

SWEDEN

Kattegat

JUTLAND
(Jylland)

Øresund

Copenhagen ✪

Store Bælt

ZEALAND
(Sjælland)

Mandø
Island

FUNEN
(Fyn)

Baltic
Sea

North
Sea

GERMANY

50 MILES

80.5 KM

© 2003 HUNTER PUBLISHING, INC.

penhagen became so rich and powerful that **King Christian IV**, after his coronation in 1596, decided to make it the economic, military, religious and cultural center of the whole of Scandinavia. To achieve this, he established trading companies with sole rights to trade overseas, and set up factories so that Denmark could become as self-sufficient as possible. The king also added two new districts to the growing city, one of which, **Christianshavn** (Christian's Harbor), is heavily influenced by the Dutch style of Amsterdam, which the king admired. Fortifications were extended to surround the new boundaries of the town. For the next two centuries everyone and everything had to enter and exit through one of four gates. Christian IV became famous for his commissioning of Dutch and German architects to produce magnificent buildings; by the time of his death in 1648 Copenhagen had been transformed into a city with grand buildings and a grand style.

The Swedish Wars

In 1657, Christian IV's successor, **King Frederik III**, declared war on Sweden, but this ended in disaster, and Denmark was forced to cede all its lands east of the Øresund; this meant that Copenhagen was no longer a city at the center of a kingdom. Two years later, despite a peace agreement, the citizens of Copenhagen only just managed to hold off the Swedes, who had conquered most of the rest of the country. These events had many consequences; the most important was that the king was able to consolidate his power against that of the nobility. Frederik III was, in 1660, acclaimed Denmark's first absolute monarch.

Much of medieval Copenhagen was burned to the ground during the fire of 1728, and strict rules regarding height, choice of materials and architectural styles were applied to the rebuilding efforts. Out of these efforts came the new Christiansborg Palace, which the king occupied in 1740; a decade later the entirely new district of Frederiksstaden, laid out in straight streets and with the beautiful palaces of Amalienborg at its center, was begun.

Rebuilding

The next 50 years brought prosperity; Denmark avoided involvement in wars and, as one of the largest naval powers, continued to defend its worldwide trade interests. The political structure also began to change. Private citizens were able to compete for wealth and status with the old nobility, and newspapers and cultural associations flourished. However, disaster was about to overtake Copenhagen. A fire in 1794 destroyed Christiansborg and large parts of the city; a few years later, during the Napoleonic Wars, England declined to accept Denmark's neutrality and attacked the Danish fleet – and the city – in the battles of Copenhagen in 1801 and 1807.

In 1813 the Danish state went bankrupt after the wars with the English, and restoration work went slowly. In order to use less space, new houses were built higher and closer together on smaller plots of land. It is somewhat ironic that this era of economic difficulty became known as the Golden Age in Copenhagen, when the arts and culture flourished. At the same time, social and economic changes caused the citizenry to become unsettled; in response, the Local Authorities Act of 1840 established a City Council, elected by and among the city's burghers, to administer more tasks. This was a forerunner to the Constitutional Act of 1849 that ended absolutism and introduced democracy. The 1840s also saw the opening of the **Tivoli Gardens** and the arrival of the **railway** in Copenhagen; the city began to expand beyond its ramparts and fortifications. In one of the most important developments, J.C. Jacobsen moved to Valby in 1847 and opened what would become an icon of Copenhagen – the **Carlsberg Brewery**. The new industries attracted many laborers from the countryside to feed the needs of the new industries and, accordingly, they began to unionize to further their demands for better living and working conditions.

The 20th Century

In 1901 the boundaries of Copenhagen were extended to the north, south and west; construction on the new, and present-day, city hall was started (this was completed in 1905), and Parliamentarism was introduced to Denmark. Seven years later women gained the right to vote in municipal elections, and a constitutional amendment extended that to universal suffrage in 1915. Denmark remained neutral during the First World War, but Copenhagen was occupied by Nazi Germany during the Second World War. Sabotage by the resistance forces, however, didn't really start until 1943 and the city escaped the war relatively unscathed.

Postwar development of Copenhagen followed the innovative **Finger Plan** of 1948; according to this plan, housing and commerce were positioned alongside radial roads and railways, which were separated by large wedges of open green space all the way in to the center of town.

As the 20th century progressed, the population began to enjoy a better standard of living, including a cradle-to-grave security that had never been experienced before. Paradoxically, the younger generation became unsettled and frequently demonstrated against nuclear weapons, NATO, the Vietnam War and their own universities. The dissent culminated, in 1971, in the creation of the **Free City of Christiania**, on the former military base of Bådsmandsstræde at Christianshavn. This community is still going strong over 30 years later, and visitors will find an established protest against generally accepted social standards. Guided tours can be arranged by calling ☎ 32-57-96-70.

The People

Among the many attractions of Copenhagen, and indeed of Denmark, the main one is, without question, the Danes themselves. Almost without exception they are friendly, charming people with a keen enjoyment of life; they value especially their family

Hygge is an untranslatable Danish word describing this attitude.

and friends, and, almost as highly, copious amounts of food and drink.

Don't be offended to find them being sarcastic with you. In fact, the more sarcastic you are in response the more they will appreciate it!

The Danes are a particularly patriotic people, and even on ordinary days visitors will be amazed to see how many Danish flags, in many variations, are in evidence. And on special public holidays, especially June 15th, Valdemar Day, the country is inundated with these images. In fact, the Danish flag, known as the *Dannebrog* (literally meaning the cloth of the Danes), is revered by the citizens, and it is also considered the oldest national – as opposed to personal – flag in the world, dating from 1219. Legend has it that, on June 15th of that year, King Valdemar II, then on a crusade to convert Estonia to Christianity, was having difficulties in a battle at Lyndanisse; a *Dannebrog* simply dropped from the sky and the king then rallied his troops to victory with it. The *Dannebrog* is commonly seen in two formats – a rectangular and a swallow tail version – and it is usually raised at sunrise and lowered at sunset. It must never touch the ground, and it is illegal to fly it at night. Dannebrog is also the name of one of two orders of chivalry, along with the Order of the Elephant, which was officially recognized by King Christian V in 1693.

Language

Pronunciation

Danish is perhaps the most difficult northern European language in terms of relating the written word to speech; it's almost impossible to pronounce simply by reading the words, as many syllables are swallowed rather than spoken. Thus, the island of Amager becomes Am-air, with the "g" disappearing, but in a distinctively Danish way difficult for foreigners to imitate. The letter "d" becomes something like a "th," but with the tongue placed behind the lower teeth, not the upper. The letter "ø" is like the "u" in English nurse, but spoken with the lips far forward. And the letter "r" is again swallowed. But don't worry; English is very widely spoken and is understood by almost everyone.

There are 29 letters in the Danish alphabet – the 26 "normal," plus "æ" (as in egg), "ø" (as in stew), and "å" (as in port). They appear after the usual 26 (a point to note when looking up names in phone books and lists).

Days of the Week

Monday	Mandag
Tuesday	Tirsdag
Wednesday	Onsdag
Thursday	Torsdag
Friday	Fredag
Saturday	Lørdag
Sunday	Søndag

Months

January	Januar
February	Februar
March	Marts
April	April
May	Maj
June	Juni
July	Juli
August	August
September	September
October	Oktober
November	November

December . . . . December

Numbers

Zero . . . . *nul*
One . . . . *en*
Two. . . . . *to*
Three . . . . *tre*
Four . . . . *fire*
Five . . . . *fem*
Six. . . . . *seks*
Seven . . . . *syv*
Eight . . . . *otte*
Nine . . . . *ni*
Ten . . . . *ti*

Climate

Denmark's relatively temperate climate is due to its geographic situation and the sea currents, but frequent switches in wind direction can bring changeable weather. Spring may come late, but summer is often sunny and autumn mild. Average monthly temperatures range from 32-33°F/0°C in January to highs of 63°F/17°C in July.

Public Holidays

Though Denmark's banks, offices, and major shops close on public holidays, museums and tourist attractions will be open, if perhaps on reduced hours. Everything will also be business as usual in the cafés.

Fixed Dates

January 1st . . . . *Nytår* (New Year's Day)
June 5th . . . . *Grundslovsdag* (Constitution Day)
June 15th. . . . . Valdemar Day

December 24th-26th .... Christmas
December 31st .... New Year's Eve

Variable Dates

Skærtorsdag.................... Maundy Thursday
Langfredag .... Good Friday
Anden påskedag................... Easter Monday
Bededag .... General Prayer Day
(fourth Friday after Easter)
Kristi himmelfartsdag .... Ascension Day
Anden pinsedag .... Whit Monday

Planning Your Trip

Entry Requirements

Americans and Canadians need only a **valid passport** to enter Denmark, and are entitled to stay for up to three months without a visa. (This includes the total amount of time spent in Denmark, Finland, Iceland, Norway, and Sweden in any six-month period.)

Making Travel Plans

Selecting Your Hotel

Really, Copenhagen doesn't have the best choice of hotels. Very few have opened in recent years, and most of those are expensive. Of the city's older properties, there are just two five-star hotels, an array of four-stars of varying quality, and a number of three-star hotels; many of the latter are clustered in the streets to the side of the railway station, a neighborhood that is not always pleasant. In general, prices are high – there are few bargains to be found, and, as is standard in Scandinavia, the rooms are often on the small side. Our price scale is based on a double room, double occupancy, and reflects the highest listed rate at the time of publication as quoted by **HORESTA** (see *The Star System*, below). But this is only an estimate, and rates can be reduced by as much as 50% at various times.

The Star System

Since 1997, all hotels that are members of the **Association of the Hotel, Restaurant and Tourism Industry** in Denmark (HORESTA), and have more than eight rooms, have been classified on a scale of one to five stars, based on specific criteria. Visit the HORESTA website, www.danishhotels.dk, to look for special rates, for information about hotel groups, and to view the criteria used in classification. A *Hotel Guide* is also available from any Danish Tourist Board office, www.visitdenmark.com.

The Copenhagen Card

The tourist office is one of the many places where you can purchase the very useful Copenhagen Card. This discount card offers unlimited travel on buses and trains in metropolitan Copenhagen and to many neighboring towns and cities; free admission to major museums and sights in and around the city; and up to a 50% discount on ferry routes connecting Zealand with Sweden and on hydrofoils between Copenhagen and Malmö. You can purchase a card that is valid for one day (DKK 155), for two days (DKK 255), or for three days (DKK 320); cards for children under 12 are available at a 50% discount. For more information, www.visitcopenhagen.dk.

Stay & Eat With The Locals

MEET THE DANES
Nyhavn, 65
☎ 33-46-46-46, fax 33-46-46-47
www.meetthedanes.com, info@meetthedanes.dk

Housed in authentic 17th-century offices at Nyhavn, this organization can help you book hotel and private accommodation, either in advance or after you arrive in Copenhagen. The group also offers, among other things, cultural lectures, dinners in private homes, and walking, cycling and sailing tours. From May 1 to mid-September, open Monday to Sunday, 9 am to 9 pm; the rest of the year, open Monday to Friday, 9 am to 6 pm; Saturday and Sunday, 10 am to 4 pm; and on holidays, 10 am to 7 pm.

What To Wear

Casual clothes are appropriate for nearly every occasion in Copenhagen, including theater and most restaurants. Only in top-class hotels, restaurants and clubs, and then not uniformly, will men be required to wear a tie in the evening; in these establishments, women do not look out of place in something dressy.

Summer evenings are long and light, but often chilly, so a **sweater** or **cardigan** is essential. Bring a lightweight **overcoat** or **raincoat**, too, in addition to ordinary summer clothes – the weather has an awkward habit of changing unexpectedly. On the beach, you can go as bare as you like.

Spring and autumn have many hours of sunshine, but cooler temperatures; and winter can be downright cold. Pack plenty of warm clothes in those seasons, plus a raincoat. Comfortable walking shoes are essential at any time of year, as it is certain you will spend a good deal of time on foot, especially in Copenhagen.

Electricity

Electric current in Denmark is **220 volts**, 50 Hz AC, and requires standard two-pin, round continental plugs. Remember to get an **adapter set** before leaving home, or at the airport.

What To Expect

Money Matters

Currency

The unit of Danish currency is the **kroner**, abbreviated kr or, abroad, **DKK** (to distinguish it from the Norwegian and Swedish kroner). It is divided into 100 øre. **Coins** are in denominations of 25 and 50 øre; and 1, 2, 5, 10, and 20 kroner. **Banknotes** are issued in denominations of 50, 100, 200, 500, and 1,000 kroner.

Banks & Exchange Bureaus

Banks and exchange bureaus offer the best rates. You pay a flat commission per transaction at banks, which are open Monday to Friday, 9:30 am to 4 pm; 6 pm on Thursday. Some branches at airports and the main railroad stations keep longer hours. Outside banking hours, exchange bureaus operate at the Central Station, the airport and other locations.

The main currency exchange agency is called **FOR-EX**, and it has offices in Copenhagen at Central Station, at N. Volgade 90 and at Nørreport 2b, and in Helsingborg and Malmö. At this writing, exchange rates are:

US $1 . . . . DKK 6.898, SEK 8.497, EURO .929
CAN $1 . . . . DKK 4.72, SEK 6, EURO .62

Credit Cards

To report lost or stolen credit cards, contact the issuing company. All of these offer 24-hour service:

American Express . . . . ☎ 80-01-00-21

Diners Club . . . . ☎ 36-73-73-73

Access, **Eurocard**, **Eurocheques**,
JCB, MasterCard and **Visa** . . . . ☎ 44-89-25-00

MOMS

Danish VAT (value added tax, or **sales tax**) is called MOMS, and is set at 25%. It's always included in the bill. For expensive purchases (a minimum purchase of 300kr in any one store) there are special tax-free export schemes. Look for shops displaying signs indicating *Europe Tax-Free Shopping* or *Tax-Free International*; retailers are well acquainted with the necessary procedures.

Health & Safety

Insurance

It is essential to have comprehensive **health insurance** coverage for your trip; your travel agent or insurance company will advise you.

Emergencies

In Denmark, **emergency treatment** (and even hospitalization) is free for any tourist taken suddenly ill or involved in an accident. For minor treatments, doctors, dentists, and drugstores will charge on the spot. Remember, you will need to pay in cash.

The all-purpose **emergency number** throughout Denmark is **112**, and is free from public phone boxes. Ask for police, fire, or ambulance. English will always be understood; speak distinctly, and state your location or the number of the phone box you are calling from.

Medications

A Danish **drugstore** (*apotek*) is strictly a dispensary. Some medicines that can be bought over the counter in other countries are available only by prescription here. Pharmacies are listed in the phone book under *Apoteker*. Normal hours are from 9 am to 5:30 pm, and until 1 pm on Saturday, though some are open 24 hours.

Telephone System

Generally, for both local and long-distance calls, **phone booths** take prepaid, disposable telephone cards that can be purchased from shops and kiosks.

Remember, calling home – or anywhere else – from your hotel room is always prohibitively expensive unless you are using a **calling card** or other means of dialing through your long distance supplier at home. It is important, though, to get the access numbers for free connections from that supplier prior to traveling, as these numbers are not always easily available once you are away from home (and they are different for each country).

The **country code** for calls to the USA and Canada is 1; to Great Britain, 44; to Australia, 61; to New Zealand, 64; to the Republic of Ireland, 353; and to South Africa, 27. The country code for calls to Denmark is 45, and the **city code** for Copenhagen is 33.

Weights & Measures

Length

1 Mile	**1.62 Km**
5 Miles	**8.1 Km**

10 Miles . . . . **16.2 Km**

Speed

20 Mph. . . . . **32 Km/h**
30 Mph. . . . . **48 Km/h**
40 Mph. . . . . **64 Km/h**
50 Mph. . . . . **80 Km/h**

Liquid Measure

1 Gallon US . . . . **3.78 Liters**
5 Gallons US . . . . **18.9 Liters**
1 Gallon UK . . . . **4.54 Liters**
5 Gallons UK . . . . **22.7 Liters**

Temperature

32° F. . . . . **0° C**
41° F. . . . . **5° C**
50° F. . . . . **10° C**
59° F. . . . . **15° C**
68° F. . . . . **20° C**
77° F. . . . . **25° C**
86° F. . . . . **30° C**

Weight

1 lb. . . . . **2.2.0 kg**
5 lbs . . . . **11.0 kg**
10 lbs . . . . **22.0 kg**

Clothing Sizes

Men's Suits & Coats
US/UK 36. . . . . **DK 46**
US/UK 38. . . . . **DK 48**
US/UK 40. . . . . **DK 50**
US/UK 42. . . . . **DK 52**

US/UK 44. . . . . DK 54
US/UK 46. . . . . DK 56

Men's Shirts
US/UK 14. . . . . DK 36
US/UK 14½ . . . . DK 37
US/UK 15. . . . . DK 38
US/UK 15½ . . . . DK 39
US/UK 16. . . . . DK 40
US/UK 16½ . . . . DK 41
US/UK 17. . . . . DK 42

Men's Shoes
US 8½-UK 8. . . . . DK 43
US 9-UK 8½. . . . . DK 44
US 9½-UK 9. . . . . DK 45
US 10-UK 9½. . . . . DK 46
US 10½-UK 10. . . . . DK 47
US 11-UK 10½. . . . . DK 48

Ladies' Dresses
US 6/UK 8 . . . . DK 40
US 8/UK 10 . . . . DK 42
US 10/UK 12 . . . . DK 44
US 12/UK 14 . . . . DK 46
US 14/UK 16 . . . . DK 48

Ladies' Shoes
US 5½-UK 4. . . . . DK 37
US 6-UK 4½. . . . . DK 38
US 6½-UK 5. . . . . DK 38
US 7-UK 5½. . . . . DK 39
US 7½-UK 6. . . . . DK 39
US 8-UK 6½. . . . . DK 40
US 8½-UK 7. . . . . DK 40

Copenhagen
A Brief History

By the 1100s the city that began as a trading post was becoming more important. At that time, the Catholic Church established cathedrals in **Roskilde** and **Lund** (the latter is in Sweden). Around the year 1160, King Waldemar gifted Copenhagen to Absalon, Bishop of Roskilde, thus giving it a status apart from others in Denmark that remained under the power of the throne.

The City Today

These days the old inner city of Copenhagen is an absolute delight to visit. Within easy walking distance from most hotels there is an eclectic collection of handsome buildings, delightful squares, imposing statues and fountains, beautiful green areas, a fantastic array of museums, enticing shopping, busy waterways, a mouth-watering collection of restaurants, and more bars and cafés than can possibly be visited. In fact, Copenhagen was named the **Cultural Capital of Europe** in 1996.

Getting Here

By Air

COPENHAGEN AIRPORT
(*Lufthavn Kastrup*)
www.cph.dk

This airport is considered to be the main air transportation hub for northern Europe, and it is one of the continent's busiest. It is about 10 kilometers (six miles) southeast of the city center, on the island of **Amager**, near the towns of Dragør and Store Magleby.

From the US & Canada

SAS
☎ 800-221-2350 or www.flysas.com

SAS (Scandinavian Airlines System) operates daily flights to Copenhagen from Newark and Chicago.

ICELANDAIR
☎ 800-223-5500 or www.icelandair.com

Icelandair has flights to and from Copenhagen from Baltimore/Washington; Boston; Halifax, Nova Scotia; New York City; and Orlando, Florida. There is a change of plane in Reykjavik, offering a great opportunity for a stopover in Iceland.

Train Connections

The fastest way from the airport to Copenhagen's city center is to take the new *Øresundstoget* (Øresund Train), a fast-train link to **Central Station**. Trains leave from Track 2 under Terminal 3, and there are three departures every hour. The trip takes just 12 minutes and costs DKK 18 each way.

Bus Connections

Buses depart about every 15 minutes to different points in the area. Bus 250S departs every 10 to 20 minutes for the **Central Station**; the trip takes 25 minutes and the fare is DKK 22.50. Other bus numbers from the airport are 9, 500S, 19, 36 and 58.

Taxi Connections

Taxis depart from outside the terminal. They take between 20 and 30 minutes to most locations in Copenhagen, and cost between DKK 120 and DKK 160.

By Boat

The large hydrofoil vessels that make the 45-minute crossing between **Copenhagen** and **Malmö, Sweden**, are docked just a few minutes walk from the town center. The one-way fare from Copenhagen is approximately DKK 52, with a 10% discount for Copenhagen Card holders. For reservations, ☎ 33-15-15-15, or www.scandlines.dk.

By Train

Service to and from Copenhagen is excellent. Trains depart from **Central Station**, adjacent to Tivoli Gardens, to just about anywhere you'll want to go in Denmark, as well as to most major cities in Europe.

S-Trains (*S-Togene* or *S-Tog*), ☎ 33-14-17-01, www.s-tog.dk, depart from platforms 9, 10, 11 and 12 at Central Station. They cover the Greater Copenhagen area that includes Helsingør, Hillerød and Roskilde. DSB trains (see below) also stop at Roskilde.

Danish State Railway (*DSB*) trains, ☎ 70-13-14-15, www.dsb.dk, operate throughout the rest of the country. **Inter-City** trains travel between the major Danish regions. **Inter City Express** (*Inter-City-Lyn*) trains travel on the same routes as the regular Inter-City trains but make fewer stops. **Regional lines** (*Regionaltogene*) connect cities throughout Zealand and the islands of Lolland and Falster.

Round-The-Sound

Four cities on the Øresund – two in Denmark and two in Sweden – are connected by ferry and train service. A Round-The-Sound ticket, available in either country, allows you to go from Copenhagen to **Malmö**, **Helsingborg** and **Helsingør**, then back to Copenhagen, by a combination of ferry, train and hydrofoil. You may begin your journey in any one of those cities and end at the city of origin, with the caveat that you always travel in the same direction. Contact the ferry lines, the railway ticket offices or the tourist bureaus for fare and schedule information.

Getting Around

On Foot

Not the least of Copenhagen's charms is that it is a fairly small city and most of its attractions, with the possible exception of the Carlsberg Brewery, the Zoo and parts of Christianshavn, are easily reached by a pleasant walk. See pages 46 and 52 for walking tour info.

By Bicycle

Bicycles are ubiquitous here and, despite the city's heavy automobile traffic, you will notice thousands of them in all shapes and sizes, some equipped with boxes on the front for carrying children or packages.

By Bus & Train

For occasions when walking is not practical, the **HT Buses** and **S-Train** (S-tog) comprise an excellent public transport system. Bus service is available between 7 am and 9:30 pm (HT, ☎ 36-13-14-15 or www.ht.dk); and electrified train service runs between 6:30 am and 11 pm (S-tog, ☎ 33-14-17-01 or www.dsb.dk). These cover not just Copenhagen but its extensive metropolitan area.

The fare system in Copenhagen is somewhat complicated. Tourists can avoid confusion by purchasing a **Copenhagen Card** (see page 10), which, along with other benefits, offers unlimited travel on buses and trains in the metropolitan area and to several destinations outside the city.

By Metro

In October of 2002, the first sections of the new Copenhagen Metro became operational, and the ticketing structure has been integrated with that of buses and S-Trains in the Greater Copenhagen area, including use of the Copenhagen Card. The Metro is fully automatic – without any train conductors; it has a top speed of 80 km/h (50 mph), and an average speed of 40 km/h (25 mph). The reality is, however, that until service is extended to the airport, most visitors will find it useful only when traveling between the city center and the major stops such as **Kongens Nytorv** and **Christianshavn**. For more information, check on-line at www.oerestadselskabet.dk/publicm.

By Car

For this guide, I have not really considered the option of traveling by car, as renting is so expensive, as is gas, and the driving regulations in Northern Europe can be very stringent. Public transportation, on the other hand, is generally very efficient.

In the event you do want to rent a car, it is much better to make the arrangements ahead of time

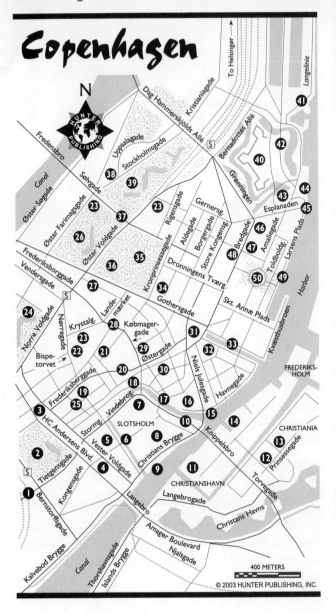

Copenhagen

N

To Helsingør →

Copenhagen Key

CHURCHES
7. Christiansborg Palace Church (*Slotskirke*)
11. Christians Church
12. Church of Our Saviour
16. Royal Navy Church (*Holmens Kirke*)
20. Church of the Holy Ghost
22. Church of Our Lady
25. Domhuset
28. Trinity Church
30. St. Nicholas Church
43. St. Albans Church
47. St. Ansgar's Church
48. Alexander Nevsky Church; Marble Church (*Marmor Kirke*)

PALACES
7. Christiansborg Palace
32. Charlottenborg; Royal Theater
36. Rosenborg Palace
40. The Citadel (*Kastellet*)
50. Amalienborg Palace Complex; Amalienborgplads

MUSEUMS
4. Ny Carlsberg Glyptotek
5. David's Collection
7. Thorvaldsen's Museum & Mausoleum
9. Royal Arsenal Museum
13. Royal Navy Museum
27. Musical History Museum
29. Museum Erotica
34. National Museum
37. Danish National Gallery
38. Hirschsprung Collection
43. Museum of Danish Resistance
46. Museum of Decorative Arts
49. Royal Cast Museum

GARDENS & PARKS
2. Tivoli Gardens
4. Winter Garden
24. Orstedsparken
26. Botanic Gardens (*Botanisk Have*)
35. King's Garden (*Kongens Have*); Rosenborg Garden
39. Østre Anlæg
42. Churchill Park

HISTORIC SITES
1. Central Station
3. Town Hall Square
6. Marble Bridge; Stables; Royal Theater Museum
8. Royal Library
10. Old Børsen
14. Old Dock (*Gammel Dok*)
15. Malmö Ferry Dock: Hydrofoil (*Flyvebådene*)
16. National Bank
17. Holmens Canal & Bridge
18. Gammel Strand; Højbro Bridge
19. Gammeltorv; Nytorv
20. Strøget
21. Grey Friars' Square
23. University (3 Locations)
28. Round Tower (*Rundeturn*)
31. Kongens Nytorv
33. Nyhavn; Nyhavn Bridge
41. Little Mermaid; *Langelinie*
44. Gefion Fountain; *Nordre Toldbold*
45. Royal Barge

S̲   S-Train Stations

············· Rail Lines

Copenhagen

through an agency. The best choices are **Auto Europe** (☎ 888-223-5555, www.autoeurope.com), **Hertz** (☎ 800-654-3131, www.hertz.com) or **Avis** (☎ 800-230-4898).

By Taxi

Taxis, and plenty of them, cruise the streets of Copenhagen; these are recognizable by a *Taxi* or *Taxa* sign, with vacant cabs displaying the word *FRI* (free). Tips are included in the meter price, but feel free to round the sum upwards if you are pleased with the service.

All taxis are radio-controlled; call ☎ 35-35-35-35 or 32-51-51-51. For a handicapped-accessible taxi or a mini-bus, ☎ 35-39-35-35. The basic fare is DKK 22, with a per-km surcharge of DKK 10 between 6 am and 3 pm; DKK 11 between 3 pm and 6 am, and on Sunday and national holidays; and DKK 13 on Friday and Saturday between 11 pm and 6 am. Keep in mind that, though taxis are plentiful, you can't always find a vacant one – especially in wet weather.

By Boat

Naturally, with the city's many canals, its wide harbor, and the presence of the Baltic Sea at hand, there are several options for both sightseeing and getting around the city on the water. These are the most popular boat tours.

DFDS transports more than 500,000 passengers a year.

Canal & Harbor Tours

DFDS offers guided tours on flat-bottomed boats, with commentary in Danish, English and German, that take you all around the harbor areas; into the canals around the Christiansborg Palace; and across the harbor to Christianshavn. The **Yellow route** begins and ends at Gammel Strand (see page 46) and the **Red route** begins and ends at Nyhavn (see page 54). The only difference between the tours is that the Yellow route doesn't actually enter Nyhavn.

Tours run from late March to late October; sailings begin at 10 am and finish at 5 pm daily, and take about 50 minutes. Between late June and late August the last departure is at 7:30 pm. The fare is DKK 50; DKK 10 less with the Copenhagen Card. For information, ☎ 32-96-30-00; to book a tour, ☎ 33-42-33-20 or www.canal-tours.dk.

Netto Boat trips start at the quayside by Holmens Church (*Holmens Kirke*, see page 42), across from the Christiansborg Palace complex, then sail out to take in Nyhavn, the Holmen area on the other side of the harbor, and the Little Mermaid; then they follow the Christianshavn and Frederiksholm's Canals back to the starting point. Tours run from the third week of March to the third week of October, between 10 am and 5 pm; the fare is DKK 20. For additional information, call ☎ 32-54-41-02 or www.netto-baadene.dk.

Netto boats
are light blue.

Water Bus

DFDS also operates a water bus system with two routes: the **Green Tour** and the **Blue Tour**. Both operate from early May to early September, and have an extended schedule between the end of May and the end of August. These tours stop at every site, and there are no guides.

The Green Tour is the most extensive; starting and ending at **Nyhavn**, it covers the canals on both sides of the harbor, goes past **The Little Mermaid** statue, and then goes out to the **Trekroner Fortress** at the entrance to the harbor.

The Blue Tour, on the other hand, starts at the **Old Dock** near Nyhavn, then sets sail for Nyhavn and the **Royal Library** (known as the Black Diamond); it crosses the harbor and makes a loop between **Islands Brygge's** new Marriott Hotel and the **Fisketorvet** shopping center, and back to Islands Brygge, before taking Holmens Canal leading to **Gammel Strand**. The tour then passes the **Christiansborg**

Copenhagen

Palace complex before heading back to Nyhavn and the Old Dock.

Tours run between May and early September, daily from 9:30 or 10 am to 5:30 or 6 pm. Tickets are DKK 30 for the Green Tour, and DKK 20 for the Blue Tour. For more flexibility, purchase a two-day transfer ticket for DKK 40; this allows you to change between tours at either Gammel Strand or the Royal Library. For information, ☎ 33-42-33-20.

The Harborbus

HT's distinctive gold and dark blue boats are operated by a partnership between HT, the City of Copenhagen, and the Port of Copenhagen, with aid from the Danish state.

HT operates the Copenhagen transportation system, and has recently introduced two Harborbuses that crisscross the harbor between **Nordre Toldbod** – the stop for the Little Mermaid – and the **library**. Line 901 sails southbound from Nordre Toldbod, and line 902 operates on the reverse route. A ticket costs DKK 24 if bought on board; note that all of the above is free with the Copenhagen Card. For additional information, call ☎ 36-13-14-15, or www.ht.dk.

Hydrofoil

Flyvebådene are the large hydrofoil vessels that make the 45-minute crossing to and from Malmö, Sweden. These are docked at the junction of Nyhavn and the harbor. The one-way fare from Copenhagen is approximately DKK 52 (fares do vary), with a 10% discount for Copenhagen Card holders. For reservations, call ☎ 33-15-15-15 or www.scandlines.dk.

Elephants of Copenhagen

One of the most surprising aspects of Copenhagen, and one not readily recognized by the Danes themselves let alone visitors to the city, is the collective presence – in many shapes, sizes and guises – of elephants.

The Order of the Elephant

One of the city's elephant manifestations can be traced back to the 1470s when King Christian I formed a brotherhood of knights, and had it confirmed by the Pope. It is thought that an elephant was chosen for the insignia of this honorary chivalric order as battle elephants were at that time a symbol of Christianity; they also represented chastity and purity. More symbolism is found in the fact that elephants carrying a tower (castle) are associated with the Virgin Mary.

It is also considered that Denmark's unique relationship with **Thailand**, where the royal family's most sacred emblem is a white, or albino, elephant, may have had an influence on the choice of insignia.

Changes in the Order

The order was still in existence during the reign of Christian II, 1513-1523, but the onset of the Reformation saw this Catholic institution lose much of its importance; it wasn't awarded again until the coronation of King Frederik II in 1559, this time with an elephant on the badge.

A century later, in 1660, absolutism was introduced in Denmark, and although this reduced many of the privileges of the old nobility they still held more residual political and economic power than King Christian V preferred. On December 1st, 1693, in an attempt to offset the influence of the old nobility, he signed statutes establishing two new royal orders of chivalry; this created a new level of nobility that would support him. One of these new orders was the Order of the Elephant (the other was the Order of the Dannebrog – see page 6); its motto is *Magni*

Thailand wanted to ally itself with a country that would not be tempted to colonize it, and it chose Denmark, which had no such intention.

Animi Pretium. The statutes fixed the maximum number of knights of the order at 30, excluding the monarch and his sons, and stated that no other forms of decoration could be worn at the same time. The monarch heads the order, which only has one class; it can be bestowed on members of the Danish royal family, foreign heads of state, and a very select few others. Only three ordinary Danish citizens were so honored during the 20th century, along with world leaders such as General Dwight Eisenhower, Field Marshal Sir Bernard Montgomery, Sir Winston Churchill, General Charles de Gaulle and Lech Walesa of Poland. Although the Order of the Elephant was presented to Queen Louise by her husband Christian IX to mark their golden wedding anniversary in 1892, and has been given to other female members of the royal family, it wasn't until April 9th, 1958, that King Frederik IX amended the statutes so that women outside the royal family would have an equal right to receive this prestigious award.

The Insignia of the Order

The insignia consists of a badge about two inches tall, made of white-enameled gold. This is in the shape of an elephant with a castle on its back, being driven by a spear-carrying Moor. The front of the elephant is decorated with a cross of diamonds, and the monogram of the issuing monarch is on the reverse.

The insignia is worn with a chain (this isn't given as part of the honor, and has to be purchased or rented by the honoree), consisting of alternating elephants and castles. The elephants have a blue cover marked with a D, representing the medieval Latin word for Denmark: *Dacia*.

The badge is worn on celebratory days such as January 1st and the reigning monarch's birthday; and on June 28th, the birthday of Valdemar II "The Victorious." On these dates, the insignia is worn in combination with an eight-pointed silver star with a central red medallion cross surrounded by laurels; this star-and-cross is worn on the left side of the chest.

On all other state occasions, the light blue silk moiré sash of the Order replaces the chain; it is draped over the left shoulder, with the elephant badge resting by the right hip.

The Order of the Elephant is bestowed only for life; upon the knight's death all insignia must be returned to the College of Arms. Examples of the various forms of the insignia are on display at the Crown Jewel exhibition in **Rosenborg Castle** (*Rosenborg Slot*: see page 36).

Elephants in Church

Another manifestation of the royal fondness for elephants can be found at **The Church Of Our Savior** (*Vor Frelsers Kirke*; see page 40) at Christianshavn. This church was in the middle of reconstruction in 1693 when Christian V made the Order of the Elephant Denmark's most prestigious honorary award. To commemorate the inauguration of the order, the king had two large ornamental elephants installed in the church; they seem to be supporting the immense organ. The high central arch of the church is decorated with the insignia of the Order of the Elephant, among other things. Vor Frelsers Kirke is known as the King's Church, as it was that monarch's first and most important monument.

Also worth seeing is the much smaller and less pretentious **Royal Navy Church** (*Holmens Kirke*), located near the **Holmens Canal** (see page 42), also favored by royalty; it is where Queen Margrethe was married in 1967. The church's elaborate metal fencework has golden elephants carrying black castles built into it.

Elephants in the Navy

In Christianshavn, hidden by the side of the canal, is the **Royal Danish Naval Museum** (*Orlogsmuseet*, see page 70), where you will find a magnificent crowned elephant head with the letter "D" engraved underneath the tusks; this head formed part of the figurehead from the ship of the line *Elephanten*, which was launched in 1741 (the ship subsequently sank in the harbor).

Elephants in Business

Unquestionably, the largest elephants (at least of the inanimate kind) can be seen some distance out of the center of the city. J.C. Jacobsen, who later became noted for his philanthropy, opened a brewery in 1847 on a hill and named it **Carlsberg** – Carl's Hill – in honor of his son (see page 4). Over 50 years later, in 1901, that same son was inspired by an obelisk at the Minerva Square in Rome. He commissioned the architect J.L. Dahlerup to design a monumental gateway for the brewery, to be supported by four massive elephants; it is made of granite from the Danish Baltic island of Bornholm.

Above the gateway of the brewery is inscribed Jacobsen's motto, Laboremus pro Patria – *Let us work for our country.*

Carlsberg's connection with elephants goes further than this gateway. In 1955, the company developed a new German-style bock (German for ram) beer to replace their Special Brew (that is still available, but only in the UK). This new beer – darker, more flavorful and stronger than most lagers – is called, naturally, *Elephant*. It is brewed under license in Canada and marketed there and in the USA under the brand name *Carlsberg Imported Elephant*. Elephant beer is sold in over 120 countries around the world. This author is pleased to personally recommend this brew, as it was his beer of choice well before he discovered these facts.

FOR BEER LOVERS

If that description fits you, then you should make tracks for the Carlsberg Visitors Center, taking either a number 6 or 18 bus from Rådhuspladsen (about a 20-minute ride); here, on Tuesday and Sunday, between 10 am and 4 pm, you can take a tour of the old brewery buildings. The tour informatively demonstrates the methods of brewing. It ends near the drayhorse stables, in a bar where you can sample the different beers produced by Carlsberg. Visitors will also have an opportunity to buy a souvenir from the new shop. Admission is free; ☎ 33-27-13-14. Take a few moments, also, to wander around the corner to **Ny Carlsberg Vej**, to see the huge stone elephants at the gate.

The swastikas on the gateway's elephants, it should be noted, were influenced by Jacobsen's interest in Eastern mythology, not politics.

By coincidence, I am sure, just across the *Søndermarken* park from the Carlsberg Brewery, is yet another place in Copenhagen where you will find elephants. But then again, the **Copenhagen Zoo** (*Zoologisk Have*, see page 81) is the one logical place in Copenhagen where you would expect to come across these charming characters. What you would not expect to find, though, if you just happened to come across it, would be the ceremony that is hosted here once a year by Carlsberg. On a particular day, the brewery invites some of its important Swedish customers to meet in the elephant house of the zoo. The ceremony calls for the drinking of an Elephant beer and bestowing upon each customer the insignia of Carlsberg's own particular Order of the Elephant – in this case a special Elephant pin!

Copenhagen

Elephant Beer

It goes without saying that Elephant beer is not in short supply in Copenhagen. But there is just one bar in the city that sells it in draft form, and then in a unique way. The bar, *Musen & Elefanten* (The Mouse & Elephant, see page 105), is a rather rough-and-ready sort of place, and very easily overlooked even if you know where it is supposed to be. In spite of this difficulty, the bar has achieved a kind of cult status among Copenhageners, and few are eager to let visitors in on their secret. At the bar, a model of an elephant's head is mounted on the wall, and the beer is drawn by pulling on a tusk; the golden, delicious and potent liquid flows through the trunk into your waiting glass.

There is another out-of-the-ordinary establishment in Copenhagen where you are able to enjoy Elephant beer. Inside the Radisson SAS Scandinavia Hotel (the tallest hotel in Denmark), you will find the city's own branch of the world-famous **Blue Elephant** restaurant chain, which specializes in Royal Thai Cuisine (see page 110). And, yes, you've guessed it, they sell their own version of bottled Elephant beer, under the Chang label. Chang, the Thai word for elephant, is Thailand's number-one selling beer, accounting for half of that country's domestic market. Thailand's Chang beer is the product of a joint venture between Chang's parent company and Carlsberg; it was launched in 1994 and is brewed under Carlsberg's supervision. It is slightly less flavorful and a little less strong than the original Danish version. Chang beer is now available in the United States, although distribution is limited.

Given the historical background, it shouldn't come as too much of a surprise to find a Thai elephant connection here.

Royal Copenhagen

The People, Not The Porcelain

The Danish monarchy is one of the world's oldest, boasting an unbroken line of 50 kings and two queens that stretches back 1,000 years. In fact, its origins have been traced back to **Gorm the Old**, who died in 958. In its earlier form the monarchy was elective, but it was not unusual for the eldest son of the reigning monarch to be chosen to succeed him. The direct line of the old dynasty ended in 1448 with the death of **Christoffer III**. Duke Christian of Oldenburg, who belonged to one of the collateral branches of the dynasty, was elected to succeed him as **King Christian I**, thus founding the House of Oldenburg. Interestingly, beginning with the election of **Frederik I** in 1523, successive monarchs have adopted the names Frederik and Christian on an alternating basis.

In 1660-1661 **King Frederik III** instituted a hereditary monarchy; this form of monarchy lasted until 1849. On June 5th of that year, **Frederik VII** signed into law a new constitution introducing a constitutional monarchy. Fourteen years later, in 1863, King Frederik died without any heirs, and this was the end of the House of Oldenburg.

According to the Act of Succession of 1853, the crown then passed into the hands of **Prince Christian of Glücksborg** who acceded as Christian IX and became the first monarch of the still-reigning **House of Glücksborg**. This king earned himself the affectionate title "the father-in-law of Europe," as three of his daughters married kings or dukes; in 1905 his grandson Carl became King of Norway.

Another Act of Succession, dating from March 1953, established the rights of succession for the heirs of

Margrethe is not the first queen of Denmark, just the first queen regnate; her namesake and predecessor, Queen Margrethe I (1353-1412), ruled on behalf of her son, Oluf.

Christian X. He died in 1947, having reigned for 35 years and through two World Wars. This Act stated that sons had precedence over daughters but, in the instance of there not being a son, the eldest daughter of the monarch would inherit the throne. This act allowed Christian's granddaughter, the current **Queen Margrethe II**, to succeed to the throne on January 14th 1972, upon the death of her father **Frederik IX**. The monarchy in general, and the queen in particular, is regarded with affection and respect by most of the citizens of Denmark. Queen Margrethe, born in 1940, is currently the world's youngest queen. She attempts to meet regularly with a wide range of people, and every two weeks holds a public audience that, in principle at least, is open to all comers.

Royal Architecture

Palaces

CHRISTIANSBORG CASTLE
(*Christiansborg Slotsplads*)
☎ 33-92-64-92

This is the most prominent royal palace in Copenhagen; it is situated on the small island of **Slotsholmen**. Several fortresses have stood on this site since Bishop Absalon commissioned the first in 1167. The present impressive neo-baroque-style palace was designed by **Thorvald Jørgensen**, who won the job by way of an architectural competition, after the previous one was destroyed by fire in 1884. It was constructed between 1907 and 1928. Its imposing copper roof is even newer, the original tiled roof having been replaced in 1937-1938. The much earlier **chapel**, the **Theater Museum**, and the **riding stables**, which managed to survive the 1884 fire, give the palace an older ambiance than its more recent origins suggest. The castle proper houses the Royal Reception Chambers (see below), the Queen's library, the audience chambers, the Sovereign-in-Council rooms, Parliament and Supreme Court chambers, as well as a complex of museums. The tower that dominates the buildings is, at 106 m (348 ft), the tallest in Copenhagen.

ROYAL RECEPTION CHAMBERS
(*Kongelige Repræsentationslokaler*)
☎ 33-92-64-92, www.ses.dk

The Royal Reception Chambers have two distinct parts; they consist of the **Royal Reception Rooms** and the **Great Hall**. These are undoubtedly a highlight of a tour of Christiansborg.

The Reception Rooms are quite grand; they include the gold and green room where monarchs are proclaimed from a balcony overlooking Castle Square (*Slotspladsen*), though Danish monarchs have not actually been crowned since the days of Christian VIII. One of your guide's first anecdotes will most probably be, "Look at the roof here, held by pillars in the shape of male statues, heads bent to take the weight – a symbol of modern Danes paying their taxes."

The Great Hall is now home to *Les Gobelins*, a series of 11 tapestries commissioned in 1990 by the Danish business community to commemorate the 50th birthday of Queen Margrethe. These elaborate and highly colorful works took such time to create, however, that they were not installed until a full 10 years later, on April 12th, 2000, at which time the Queen donated them to the state. The tapestries are impressive indeed, and are accompanied by detailed outlines describing just exactly what each individual section represents.

Only one section is open at any given time, and tours have varying hours; it is best to consult *Copenhagen*

The Royal Reception Chambers are very formal, and strict rules are enforced. For example, in order to protect the highly valuable parquet floors, canvas slippers are provided for visitors to wear over their shoes before joining a guided tour.

This Week (see page 130) for opening hours during your visit. Tours of the Great Hall are given only in Danish. Admission is DKK 45.

BORG RUINS OF ABSALON'S PALACE
(*Ruinerne af Absalons*)
☎ 33-92-64-92, www.ses.dk

Underneath Christiansborg palace are the extensive, well-preserved brick and stone ruins of the site's previous structures, including Bishop Absalon's citadel of 1167; these ruins were carefully protected during the construction of the present palace. From May to September open daily, 9:30 am to 3:30 pm; from October to April, open Tuesday, Thursday, Saturday and Sunday during the same hours. Admission is DKK 20, free with the Copenhagen Card.

ROSENBORG CASTLE
(*Rosenborg Slot*)
☎ 33-15-32-86

In the early 17th century, Christian IV decided that Christiansborg Palace was too official and oppressive for his tastes. Accordingly, he commissioned *Rosenborg Have*, a very charming park, which was laid out between 1606 and 1634; in a corner of the park, then located outside the city walls, he ordered the construction of a small mansion. This he eventually expanded into a most charming and delightful three story Dutch-Renaissance-style palace. Although its design incorporates towers, moats and battlemented gateways – those attributes expected in a typical castle – it has retained the ambiance of a weekend retreat. The next three generations of kings used Rosenborg as their home, but after 1710, subsequent to Frederik IV's construction of Frederiksberg Castle, it was used only occasionally by the royal family.

Since 1838 Rosenborg has housed a museum of considerable grace and character, with exhibits spanning 500 years of Danish royal history. Its 24 rooms are arranged chronologically, beginning with Christian IV's tower study – still furnished in its original Renaissance style – and culminating with the magnificent **Long Hall**, with its Swedish Wars tapestries dating from 1685, ornate ceiling, three near-life-size silver lions, and one of the world's largest collections of silver furniture (most dating from the 18th century). Exhibits of particular note include the Rosenborg Tapestries, which were woven in the late 17th century, and which were returned here from Christiansborg Slot in early 1999.

The Danish crown jewels are on view in the treasury, which is in the cellar; here, in addition to the oldest existing specimen of the insignia of the Order of the Elephant, you will find numerous cases displaying crowns, gilded swords, precious stones, coronation cups, royal inkwells, tea-sets and other objects of pure gold. The highlight, though, is the 17th-century crown of the absolute monarchy; it is fashioned from gold and set with diamonds, two sapphires, and ruby spinels.

Rosenborg is open from November to mid-December and from January to April, Tuesday to Sunday, 11 am to 2 pm; in May and June, daily, 10 am to 4 pm; from July through September, daily, 10 am to 5 pm; and in October, daily, 11 am to 3 pm. Admission DKK 50, but a discount is available with the Copenhagen Card.

AMALIENBORG PALACE
(Amalienborg Plads)

These days, when the royal family is in Copenhagen its home is at Amalienborg. The complex consists of four separate palaces around an octagonal plaza. Four boulevards converge on this open space, and

Copenhagen

bearskin-hatted soldiers, stationed in tall, pencil-thin guard boxes with pointed roofs, guard each of the palaces. Dominating the center of the plaza is a huge equestrian statue of Frederik V, which took 20 years to fashion and was unveiled to a 27-gun salute in 1771. Initially, the plan was to celebrate the 300th jubilee of the Oldenburg dynasty, and the square's design celebrates the French baroque style popular during that time. Collectively known today as Amalienborg Palace, and named in honor of Queen Sophie Amalie, the wife of Frederik III, these buildings are considered to be among the finest examples of rococo architecture in Europe.

With four identical mansions around its octagonal perimeter, Amalienborg is considered to be one of the most attractively symmetrical squares in Europe.

The palaces were built originally as residences for prominent aristocratic families. However, after Christiansborg castle was destroyed by fire for a second time in 1794, the royal family bought up Amalienborg from the nobles, and have lived here since. Presently, the Queen resides in Frederik VIII's palace, on the left as you enter the square. Then, going clockwise, the royal family lives in the palace of Christian IX; Christian VII's palace is used for visiting dignitaries; and the fourth, which houses the Amalienborg Palace Museum (see below), is known as Christian VIII's palace.

AMALIENBORG PALACE MUSEUM
☎ 32-12-08-08

Here, you can see for yourself how opulently the Danish royal family lived between 1863 and 1947. Collections include luxurious furniture, paintings, crystal and silver. The museum is open January to April, and November and December, daily except Monday, 11 am to 4 pm; and May through October, daily, 10 am to 4 pm. Admission DKK 35.

THE CHANGING OF THE GUARD

Try to time your visit to take in Amalienborg's most popular attraction, the changing of the **Royal Life Guards**. At 11:30 each morning these guards, whose principal duty is to guard the Queen at Amalienborg Palace, leave their barracks near Rosenborg Castle and march through the back streets of the city. They arrive just before noon in the palace square, where they move from one sentry-box to another in a series of foot-stamping ceremonies. When the monarch is in residence, the Guardsmen, wearing white-striped blue trousers and highly polished boots, the fur of their black bearskin hats rippling in the breeze, are accompanied by a full band; on ceremonial occasions they also wear red tunics with white shoulder straps. On April 16th, the present Queen's birthday, thousands of spectators gather here to celebrate with her and watch the noon ceremony.

Churches

CHRISTIANSBORG PALACE CHURCH
(*Christiansborg Slotskirke*)
Prins Jørgens Gård
☎ 33-92-63-00

Located on the corner of Slotsholmen, adjacent to Christiansborg Palace, and close to the **Højbro Bridge**, its original incarnation was that of a palace chapel; it had a distinguished rococo interior, dating from the mid-18th century. However, most of that structure was destroyed by fire in 1794. The replacement – in the neoclassical style with a dome top – was consecrated on May 14th, 1826, to commemorate the millennial anniversary of the introduction of Christianity to Denmark. This one was spared in an 1884 palace fire, but on June 7th, 1992, it did succumb. Although no original plans existed, an enormous effort was made to reconstruct the church, and it was reconsecrated on January 14th, 1997, to coincide with the celebration of Queen Margrethe II's silver jubilee. It was used until 1926 as Court Church for the royal family, and a mass is celebrated here in connection with the annual opening of parliament, but these days its main official purpose is to be the place where monarchs are laid in state. The church is open every Sunday from midday to 4 pm; and at Easter during the same hours.

CHURCH OF OUR SAVIOR
(*Vor Frelsers Kirke*)
Sankt Annægade 29
Christianshavn
☎ 33-54-68-83 or www.vorfrelserskirke.dk

This brick and sandstone church is known as the **King's Church**, as Christian V was its sponsor and protector, and it was his first and most important monument; indeed, it was he who dedicated the church upon its completion on April 19th, 1696.

Vor Frelsers Kirke is also affectionately known as *Grundtvigs* in honor of a Danish clergyman, poet and religious radical in his time as pastor here from 1822 to 1826; he is also known for his numerous hymns and songs; and as the People's Church, because it has always been open to a wide cross-section of the population.

Construction began in 1682 under the direction of Lambert van Haven. King Christian V, having made the Order of the Elephant Denmark's most prestigious distinction in 1693, insisted on the inclusion of elephants as a motif, and there are two quite different elephant images in the church. By the doors are two large ornamental elephants; these appear to be supporting the huge organ, which dates from 1700 (it has been remodeled several times since). Elephant images also appear on the high central arch, which is decorated with the monogram of Christian V, together with the royal coat of arms and a chain of the Order of the Elephant. Look, also, for the choir screen guarded by six wooden angels; the ornate white marble font supported by four cherubs; and the altar, dating from 1732, which is replete with allegorical statues and Dresden-like figures playing in the clouds.

All of the above notwithstanding, it is the church's external spiral staircase, dedicated in August 1752, which arouses the most curiosity. Lauridz de Thurah, inspired by the Sant'Ivo alla Sapienza church in Rome, designed this staircase, which twists its way up and around the tower four times. The stair consists of a series of 400 steps, 150 of which are on the outside, leading from the entrance of the church to the gilt globe (2.5 m/8.2 ft in diameter) and Christ figure (3 m/9.8 ft tall) atop the church's spire (this figure represents the victory of Christianity in the 17th century. From ground level to the top of the flag it is a distance of 90 m (295 ft), making it almost three times as high as the Round Tower (see page 47). King Frederik V, who was in attendance at the 1752 dedication, climbed all the way to the top. These days, visitors are only allowed the experience of this outdoor climb between April and October – and that is subject to good weather.

From November to March, the church is open Monday to Saturday, 11 am to 3:30 pm; and Sunday, midday to 3:30 pm. From April to August, hours are Monday to Saturday, 11 am to 4:30 pm; and Sunday, midday to 4:30 pm. In September and October, hours are Monday to Saturday, 11 am to 3:30 pm; and Sunday, midday to 3:30 pm. Admission DKK 20 or free with the Copenhagen Card.

Copenhagen

ROYAL NAVY CHURCH
(Holmens Kirke)
Holmens Canal
☎ 33-13-61-78 or www.holmenskirke.dk

The nave of this church was originally constructed between 1562-63 as an anchor forge for the naval dockyard. It was converted into a sailors' church in 1619 by Christian IV; its two wings were added between 1641 and 1643. Small and intimate, with a warm ambiance, this church remains a favorite with the royal family, as demonstrated in 1967, when it was chosen for the wedding of Queen Margrethe II to Prince Henrik (he was formerly the French Comte de Laborde de Montpezat). This is Copenhagen's only Renaissance-style church, and the exceptionally beautiful interior retains most of its original features, as it has managed to escape damage from fire or war over the centuries. Most notable are the altar and pulpit, both dating from the 1660s; it also has two model **votive ships** hanging from the ceiling – a strong tradition common in many Danish, and other Scandinavian, churches. The elephant motif is manifested in the golden elephants carrying black castles on their backs, which are built into the elaborate metal exterior fencework. Opening hours are Monday to Friday, 9 am to 2 pm; and Saturday, 9 am to midday. Admission is free.

Votive ships, common in churches all over Scandinavia, are meant to symbolize human life from the cradle to the grave.

Historic Buildings

DANISH ROYAL LIBRARY
(Det Kongelige Bibliotek)
Søren Kierkegaards Plads1
☎ 33-47-47-47 or www.kb.dk

The Royal Library, now housed in an attractive, traditional-style building dating from 1906, was actually founded by King Frederik III around 1653. In 1989 this library was merged with the University Library, which was founded even earlier, in 1482.

However, the main interest these days is in the surprising contrast in architectural style between the older structure and the library's new extension, which has a favorable position along the harbor. This building, affectionately dubbed the Black Diamond because of the color of the Zimbabwean granite used in its construction, is an extremely modern, seven-story, glass, granite, concrete and steel structure that appears to be leaning over the water. At night, because of its shape and color, the head- and tail lights of cars reflect on it and appear to be moving diagonally across its surface. It doubles, also, as something of a social center, hosting concerts, lectures and other meetings and housing stores, restaurants and cafés. Take the time to relax in the Library Gardens, a veritable oasis of peace and calm. The gardens are open 6 am to 10 pm; the library is open Monday to Friday, 10 am to 9 pm.

ROYAL STABLES
(*Kongelige Stalde og Kareter*)
Christiansborg Ridebane 12
☎ 33-40-26-76

As you might expect, the stables are near the vast parade ground – dominated by a copper equestrian statue of Christian IX – at the end of the U-shaped Christiansborg Palace complex. They are housed in one of the older buildings that survived the ruinous fire of 1884. The stable complex is comprised of three sections: the **Coach Hall**, which has state coaches and carriages; the actual **Stables**, housing the royal family's carriage and saddle horses; and the **Harness Room**, which features uniforms and harnesses. Open from January to April, and from October to December, Saturday and Sunday, 2 pm to 4 pm; and from May to September, Friday through Sunday, 2 pm to 4 pm. Admission DKK 20, or free with the Copenhagen Card.

The Royal Stables' Coach Hall even has an old stately Rolls Royce.

THEATER MUSEUM
(*Teatermuseet*)
☎ 33-11-51-76

The Theater Museum is in the old Court Theater, which dates from 1767; exhibits trace the history of Danish theater from the 18th century to the present. The museum is above the royal stables, with its entrance on the left-hand side. Open Wednesday, 2 pm to 4 pm; and Saturday and Sunday, midday to 4 pm. Admission DKK 20, or free with the Copenhagen Card.

DANISH ROYAL THEATER
(*Det Kongelige Teater*)
☎ 33-69-69-69
www.kgl-teater.dk

Hans Christian Andersen tried, unsuccessfully, to become a ballet dancer at the Danish Royal Theater.

This is the grandest building on Kongens Nytorv. It was inaugurated as the **King's Theater** on December 18th, 1748, and was rebuilt in 1774. At that time it was designated a theater of multiple arts. It kept its name following the abolition of absolutism in 1849, as the monarch retained the right to make free use of the theater's royal box and other seats, but its management changed significantly. In that era it lost its monopoly on entertainment as other popular theaters opened. In an effort to remain competitive, the Royal Theater inaugurated a new building on October 15, 1874. The theater complex is now home to the **Royal Danish Ballet**, the **Royal Danish Opera** and the **Royal Danish Orchestra**, and it is considered Denmark's most important cultural center. Outside the main entrance are two statues. The one on the left depicts Adam Oehlenschläger, an author of tragedies. Across from him is the image of Ludvig Holberg, a satirist whose comedic works are still popular.

THE ROYAL BARGE
Café Lumskebugten
Esplanaden, 21
☎ 33-15-60-29

The pictures of yachts displayed on the walls of this fine restaurant (see page 125) give a clue to its important role. Through a quirk of fate, the restaurant's owners have been given responsibility for operating the royal barge, which is docked here. This means that, during the summer months, two people remain on standby to ferry the Queen whenever she wants to go to and from larger vessels.

THE ROUND TOWER
(*Rundetaarn*)
Købmagergade, 52a
☎ 33-73-03-73 or www.rundetaarn.dk

The tower was built between 1637 and 1642, during the reign of King Christian IV. It forms part of a complex that also includes **Trinity Church** (*Trinitatis Kirke*; see page 76). The building has the distinction of housing the oldest preserved astronomic observatory in Europe; it functioned as the university observatory until as recently as 1861. In 1870, the original octagonal observatory was replaced; the present observatory – with a revolving dome that can be turned by hand – was built in 1929. These days it is open for use by amateur astronomers and for visitation by the general public. The tower also boasts an interior spiral ramp, unique in European architecture; this is 209 m (687 ft) in length, 4¼ m (13.94 ft) wide, and winds 7.5 turns around the hollow core of the tower. This ramp is far more practical than steps for raising heavy equipment to the observatory located above the 34.8-m (114.2-ft) summit.

Among the Round Tower's many famous guests was Russian Czar Peter the Great who, in 1716, rode to the top of the ramp on his horse, followed by his empress in a coach-and-six.

From June 1 to August 31, the Round Tower is open Monday to Saturday from 10 am to 8 pm; and Sunday, midday to 8 pm. From September 1 to May 31 it is open Monday to Saturday, 10 am to 5 pm; and Sunday, midday to 5 pm. Admission to the tower is DKK 15, or free with the Copenhagen Card. The Observatory is open June 20 to August 10, Sunday, 1 pm to 4 pm; and October 15 to March 22, Tuesday and Wednesday, 7 pm to 10 pm.

CENTRAL RAILWAY STATION
Banegårdspladsen

The royal family has its own apartment in the station, where they can wait in comfort and privacy for their train; this gives the Central Station perhaps the most esoteric royal connection in Copenhagen.

Sunup To Sundown

Walking Tour: To Gammel Strand

We begin this walking tour at **Town Hall Square** (*Rådhuspladsen*), one of the two social centers in Copenhagen – Nyhavn being the other. This central square is a popular meeting place, similar to Trafalgar Square in London and Times Square in New York. You will find transportation to and from Rådhuspladsen to be convenient; it is just across from **Tivoli Gardens** (see page 59), and is the stopping point for the most important city bus routes. Central Station, from which trains depart for destinations outside of Copenhagen, is just a few minutes walk away.

Rådhuspladsen offers the first-time visitor a fascinating insight into the Danish character. This large, open square is dotted with cafés, fruit vendors and vegetable stalls. You will also find here more than one variation on the ubiquitous hot-dog stands (*pølsevogn*) that can range in size from a simple kiosk to a small hut. These stands, where tasty, inexpensive sausages are served in a variety of forms, are an almost obligatory part of Danish life.

Public Art

Copenhagen, as you will quickly realize, is not lacking in statues. Take a few moments before you begin your walking tour to wander around the square, taking in some of the impressive examples found here. Of course, you would expect there to be a bronze version of Denmark's favorite son, storyteller **Hans Christian Andersen**; you'll find it near the eight-lane boulevard that bears his name. Look on the same side of the square for the more dramatic copper **Bull and Dragon Fountain**, dating from 1923; it depicts a fierce, watery battle between the two beasts.

Crossing to the opposite side of the square to Vester Voldgade you will find a column that has been home, since 1914, to the altogether more lighthearted **Lur Blowers** statue. Local tradition has it that the two ancient men on top will sound a note on their instruments if a virgin passes by. Given, however, that many of the Danish women you will see are somewhat more than simply attractive, it's hardly surprising that these gentlemen have led a life of silence.

Look across from Rådhuspladsen and down Vesterbrogade for an unusual monument in the middle of the street; this is the **Freedom Pillar**, erected between 1792 and 1797 to commemorate the end of serfdom for the Danish peasantry in 1788.

Town Hall

The red brick Rådhuset, constructed between 1892 and 1905, is the dominant structure here, with a formidable square tower that rises to a height of 105.6 m (346.5 ft). On the roof are six bronze figures

Copenhagen

of **night watchmen**, which date from various periods of the city's history. Approaching the building by way of a series of wide steps, the site of frequent concerts, note the copper and 22-carat gilt statue above the main doorway that is a likeness of the city's founder, **Bishop Absalon**. Once inside, you will find an architectural hodgepodge, as each section of the Town Hall has its own unique style.

Stop first just inside the main entrance where, to the left, tickets may be purchased for the three attractions within the Rådhuset – the Town Hall proper, the **City Hall Tower**, and Jens Olsen's intriguingly eccentric **World Clock**, which is encased in a huge glass cabinet. As to the first, I would suggest a guided tour, offered for DKK 30, which will allow you to see, among other things, the main hall, the imposing banqueting room with its statuary and coats-of-arms, and an impressive view of the 44 m (145 ft) hall from the first floor colonnade. On Monday through Friday these tours begin at 3 pm, and on Saturday at 10 and 11 am.

The more energetic, and those wanting a birds-eye perspective of Copenhagen, can take on the 300 steps of the City Hall Tower. This tour, which costs DKK 20, is offered between June and September, Monday through Friday, at 10 am, midday and 2 pm; and on Saturday at midday (other times of the year, visit Monday through Saturday at midday). The Town Hall Information Office (*Rådhusoplysningen*) is open Monday to Friday from 10 am to 4 pm; and Saturday, between 10 am and 1 pm. Admission DKK 10; ☎ 33-66-25-82 or www.copenhagencity.dk.

Strøget

Strøget, pronounced stroyet, means walking street.

Among Copenhagen's many claims to fame is the world's longest pedestrian-only shopping street. It is called, but not officially named, *Strøget*, and it is not a single street but rather a convergence of four separate boulevards. Beginning near Rådhuspladsen they are **Frederiksberggade**, **Nygade Vimmelskaftet**, **Amergertorv** and **Østergade**.

The entrance to Frederiksberggade, just across from Rådhuspladsen, is not exactly inviting; after all, the presence of a Burger King and a 7-Eleven, with a McDonalds just a little farther on, isn't particularly exciting. But press on and things will improve.

Note the site currently occupied by the Club Absalon. Although the fact is not widely known or readily apparent, the basement of this club is reportedly the spot where Bishop Absalon built **St. Clemens Church** in 1160. That structure was, however, demolished in the early 16th century.

At the point where Frederiksberggade becomes Nygade Vimmelskaffet, Strøget opens into two squares. To the left is **Gammeltorv**, a popular place for small market stalls and home to the **Caritas Fountain** – the city's oldest, dating from 1610. Should you happen to visit here on April 16th, the monarch's official birthday, don't be surprised to see golden apples (imitation ones, of course) dancing atop the fountain's water jets – an interesting local tradition which dates from the golden wedding anniversary of King Christian IX and Queen Louise in 1892.

The square to the right, **Nytorv**, is dominated by the old Town Hall, a very impressive, colonnaded building that now houses the **Law Courts**. This, the quieter of the two squares, offers an opportunity to partake of some refreshment at one of its street cafés and enjoy watching passers by.

From here, follow Nygade Vimmelskaftet to where it becomes Amergertorv; leaving Strøget, make a left turn into **Klosterstræde**, which will eventually lead you into the charming **Gråbrødretorv** (Grey Friars' Square). This is a picturesque square that has a large plane tree and fountain surrounded by

Copenhagen

brightly painted 18th-century houses. Prior to the Reformation it was the site of a Franciscan monastery; cafés and restaurants have proliferated here in recent years. One of the best, at number 21, is actually named after the square (see page 127).

Between early June and early September, any night from Tuesday to Saturday, return to Grey Friars' Square at 9 pm to join the **Night Watchman** on his evening rounds. These walks last one hour; no booking is necessary, but donations are expected at the end.

Just a few minutes walk away is the **Round Tower** (see page 45), one of Copenhagen's most popular attractions. To get there, take a left on Niels Hemmingsens Gade, a right on Skindergade, and a jog to the left on Købmagergade.

STUDENT HOUSING

The strangely shaped building across Købmagergade from the Round Tower is the university hostel. Although students have lived here since 1623, most of the present structure dates from the 18th century, with the exception of the notable arcade, added in 1909.

Retrace your steps along Købmagergade, away from the Round Tower to the left, and enjoy the ambiance of this wide pedestrian shopping street. Along the way you will pass **Ole Jensen Aps** delicatessen at number 32 (see *Shop Till You Drop*, page 96) and the **Museum Erotica** at number 24 (see page 68), both on the left-hand side, before continuing across Strøget into **Højbro Plads**. In the 19th century this plaza, a cross between a square and a street, was used as a fruit and flower market. Although boasting nothing of real architectural note, this is still worth a visit. The spire of **St. Nicholas Church** towers to the left, and an outdoor café sits almost directly underneath a powerful green copper equestrian statue of the warrior-priest Bishop Absalon, clad in chain mail and wielding an axe. Here, too, you get a first glance of both the canal and the imposing towers of the Christiansborg Palace, situated on the small island of Slotsholmen, on the opposite bank across the Højbro Bridge. Its attractions are described in *Royal Copenhagen* (see page 35).

Undoubtedly, your attention will be drawn across the canal to a copper-roofed building to the left of the palace. This is the **Stock Exchange** (*Børsen*). In 1619, Christian IV, ever influenced by the Dutch architecture of his day, commissioned two Dutch brothers to design a highly ornamented home for the exchange. It is graced by a famous spire composed of four intertwining dragon's tails; these are topped by three crowns symbolizing the friendship of the three Scandinavian countries of Denmark, Norway and Sweden (Finland is not considered to be part of Scandinavia). These days, the building hosts special events, while the financial movers and shakers ply their trade in their new headquarters on Strøget.

Gammel Strand

On the near side of the bridge there are two water-related statues, one of which is not immediately visible. Look over the side of Højbro Bridge to find the **Mermaid with Seven Sons** playing hide-and-seek with tourists from its home beneath the water. This is best seen at night, when it is attractively illuminated.

On the corner of Gammel Strand and Højbro Plads stands the **Fishwife** (*Fiskerkone*), erected in 1940. Dressed in a headscarf, shawl, and stout apron, she is clasping a fish. This public art is more than symbolic, as a water pump by its side indicates. For over 800 years the city's fishmongers – traditionally women – have worked from this point. It may seem, today, a strange place for fishmongers to work, but there is a reason for it. Gammel Strand means "old beach"; this is where the coastline was in the early Middle Ages, and the area has been associated with the water and fish ever since. Today, though, there is only one stall remaining; it is open Tuesday from 9:45 am to 1:30 pm; and Wednesday, Thursday and Friday from 9:45 am to 2:30 pm.

These days, Gammel Strand is a popular place for dining establishments and bars, including the ultra-elegant **Krogs** (see *Restaurants*, page 123), the city's finest seafood restaurant and the first to boast a sommelier. The strand is also home to a **flea market** every Saturday morning, as well as being one of the two principal starting-points for **canal boat tours**, the other being in Nyhavn (see *Canal & Harbor Tours*, page 24). And, immediately across the canal is a distinctive, square-arched, yellow-ochre building with a Classical-style frieze; for more information about this monument to the great Danish sculptor **Bertel Thorvaldsen**, see *Museums*, page 64.

There really is no set route from here back to Rådhuspladsen, as the maze of narrow streets is home to an untold number of antique stores, boutiques and other such places, as well as tempting restaurants, cafés and bars; just meander and explore whatever attracts your attention.

Walking Tour: To Churchill Park

From the Rådhuspladsen, follow Strøget past the point where Nygade Vimmelskaftet becomes Amergertorv. the first place of note is the **Church of the Holy Ghost** (*Helligåndskirke*; see *Churches*, page 73). The area outside its low metal fence is popular with street performers and chess players. There are also some fruit and vegetable stalls and other vendors, making a beguiling combination for this most cosmopolitan of streets.

Just beyond Helligåndskirke, Strøget opens out yet again. Until the middle of the 19th century this open place – **Amagertorv** – was a market square where the farmers and peasants of Amager sold their products. These days it is still a gathering place, but now it's a social one. People love to meet around the central **Stork Fountain** (*Storkespringvandet*) and sit at the outside tables of the surrounding bars and cafés, while being entertained by street performers. On the left-hand side of Amagertorv Square is a magnificent assortment of Dutch baroque façades. Several belong to the **Royal Copenhagen** group of stores, and others to **Illum**, a department store. Undoubtedly, the most beautiful is that belonging to Royal Copenhagen Porcelain at number 6 (see *Shop Till You Drop*, page 94).

The last street comprising Strøget is Østergade, and you will be certain to identify world famous brand names in the shop windows. Everyone is encouraged to check out the window of **Halberstadts** (page 97).

Strøget ends at the dramatic **Kongens Nytorv**. The name translates as "the king's new square," although it can be said to be new only in comparison to Denmark's very long history. It was laid out some 300 years ago, and the aim was to form a link between the old and new parts of Copenhagen. Dominating the central green area, known as **Prinsen**, is a powerful equestrian statue of Christian V, which was erected in 1688. It consists of four figures seated submissively under his horse. These days the square is undergoing extensive renovations, and a station for the new Metro line is being constructed adjacent to the Magasin department store (see page 89). Kongens Nytorv is Copenhagen's largest square. It has no less than 12 streets radiating from it, as well as a number of stately buildings surrounding it, including the **Danish Royal Theater** (see page 44).

Looking around the square, you'll notice a number of other fine buildings. Undoubtedly, the impressive façade of the five-star **Hotel d'Angleterre**, Copenhagen's – and Denmark's – finest, stands out; **Thott's Mansion** (*Thotts Palæ*) in the northeast corner, built for the naval hero **Admiral Niels Juel** and now serving as the French Embassy, is not to be overlooked either. Also interesting is a quaint triangular building, the beautifully preserved 1782 **Kanneworffs Hus**, standing between Store Strandstræde and Bredgade. The house, fronting the south side of Nyhavn and adjacent to Kongens Nytorv, is said to be the most important work of pure baroque architecture remaining in Denmark today. It was erected between 1672 and 1683 by Ulrik Frederik Gyldenløve, an illegitimate son of King Frederik III, and subsequently named **Charlottenborg** when Queen Charlotte Amalie came to reside here in 1700. This red brick Dutch baroque house, designed by native architect Evert Janssen, has had a great impact on architectural style in Denmark; many country mansions of that era were modeled in its style. Since 1754 the house has served as the seat of the **Royal Danish Academy of Art**.

The Canal

In the late 17th century, around 1671, King Frederik III wanted to extend marine commerce into the center of the city. A canal was dug perpendicular to the harbor and stretching all the way to Kongens Nytorv. Merchants were encouraged to build their houses, offices and warehouses along the banks of the **Nyhavn**, which literally means "new harbor." These plans succeeded beyond all expectations; soon, vessels from all over the world arrived, carrying not only their merchandise but also hungry, thirsty and often rambunctious sailors. Not surprisingly, many of the houses along the new harbor were transformed into bars and restaurants to meet their more urgent needs. This state of affairs continued until very recently, when the maritime trade ceased. These days (especially on the north side of the canal, now mostly a pedestrian precinct), many of the magnificent multi-colored 17th- and early 18th-century houses contain an eclectic mix of **antiques** and **specialty stores**, along with **restaurants** and **bars**. Many of these establishments are crammed with tables, and several have an outside bar serving the overflow of customers. On pleasant summer evenings and weekends there can be thousands of people who are only too happy to eat, drink and socialize along the sidewalk and quayside.

The houses are not the sole attraction, however. Enhancing the ambiance is a motley collection of sailing vessels, almost all flying a *Dannebrog*, bobbing in the water from one end of the quay to the other. In fact, it has become a summer tradition for old sailing ships, often meticulously restored, to set their sails and head for a berth at Nyhavn.

Arriving at the city end of the canal you are greeted by steps leading down to the water; nearby is a sizeable old anchor that proudly and symbolically memorializes the 1,600 Danish sailors killed in World War II. From here, it is fun to stroll down the busy north side, simply enjoying the activity and bustle. Note the coat of arms over number 67; upon further investigation you will learn that Hans Christian Andersen lived here between 1845 and 1864. Prior to that he lived at number 20, and during his final years, 1873-1875, his residence was at number 18; both of those houses are on the more sedate Charlottenborg (south) side of the canal.

The Nyhavn Canal can be considered a unique illustration of the contrasts between old and present-day Copenhagen.

At the foot of Nyhavn, by the harbor, you will see **hydrofoil** vessels moored, waiting to depart on the 45-

minute trip to Malmö, Sweden. From here you can also enjoy fine views out over the inner harbor to Christianshavn, where the unusual spiral steeple of **Vor Frelsers Kirke** dominates. Follow **Kvæsthusgade** to **Skt. Annæ Plads**, a fine boulevard lined with consulates and distinguished old offices, and then follow the quayside past the ferry dock. This is for the huge **DFDS ferry** that crosses to and from Oslo, a 16-hour trip with vessels departing both cities daily at 5 pm; the smaller ferry that travels to the Danish island of Bornholm docks on the harbor itself.

This area has been improved in recent years. The long waterside promenade passes a warehouse that has been tastefully converted into the **Admiral Hotel** (see page 115). Beyond the hotel you arrive at the long, narrow rectangular **Amaliehavn Gardens**, which were designed by the Belgian landscape architect Jean Delogne using French limestone and Danish granite. The bronze pillars that surround the fountain were designed by the Italian sculptor **Arnaldo Pomodoro**. Immediately behind the gardens are the palaces of the **Amalienborg** complex (see *Royal Copenhagen*, page 37), one of which is the home of Queen Margrethe II. Beyond the palace is the unmistakable dome of the Marble Church (see page 75). Continuing along on the promenade you pass the very unusual **Royal Cast Collection** (see *Museums*, page 65), before making a left turn onto the **Esplanaden**. Here, you might want to stop at the unusual **Lumskebugten Café**, an absolutely charming restaurant and bar that has the distinction of being keeper of the Royal Barge.

The Esplanade leads to **Churchill Park** (*Churchillparken*) and the entrance to ***Langelinie***, a promenade that runs along the harbor, as well as the **Museum of the Danish Resistance** (*Frihedsmuseet*; see *Museums*, page 70) and the British Victorian Gothic **St. Albans Church** (see *Churches*, page 76). You'll want to explore those, and to admire the park's impressive and formidable **Gefion Fountain**. Copenhagen has numerous fountains, but this is undoubtedly the most spectacular in the city. Commissioned by the Carlsberg Foundation, sculptor **Anders Bundgaard's** depiction of the Nordic goddess Gefion was unveiled in 1908. Legend has it she turned her four sons into oxen and used them to plow the island of Zealand out of Sweden. Langelinie is certainly a pleasant place to stroll, and a pavilion of the same name provides a good place to take refreshments. There is also a series of statues along Langelinie, including likenesses of Marie, Princess of Denmark, and Frederick IX, King of Denmark from 1947 to 1972. None, though, is as famous as the one statue that has become the symbol of the city.

The Little Mermaid

A few hundred meters south of the quay is *Den Lille Havfrue*, high on the "must see" list for all visitors to Copenhagen. You will find, however, that the clever angles employed in most promotional photographs make it appear, deceptively, much larger and more strategically situated than it really is. This may cause some disappointment. Nonetheless, its history is interesting, if far from idyllic.

In 1909, the brewer Carl Jacobsen, so prominent in the life of Copenhagen, attended a ballet named *The Little Mermaid*, which was based on the Hans Christian Andersen fairy tale of the same name. In this tragic story, a sea-girl exchanged her voice for human legs in order to gain the love of an earthly prince, but had to watch mutely as he jilted her for a real princess. In desperation, she threw herself into the sea, turning into foam.

Being suitably impressed by the story, Jacobsen commissioned **Edvard Eriksen** to create a sculpture of a mermaid – which he did, using his wife as the model. The resulting bronze statue was unveiled on August 23rd, 1913. Fortunately, someone had the foresight to retain the cast, which has been used for restoration on several occasions. Sadly, acts of vandalism have seen the original decapitated twice and her arm amputated once. Not much respect, then, for fairy tales in the late 20th century!

The Citadel

Follow Langelinie around to the left. You'll see a large marina to the right; take the steps down to a small wooden bridge on the left. This leads over a moat to a fortification known as the Citadel (*Kastellet*). This fort, which was a cornerstone of Christian IV's defenses of Copenhagen, was built between 1662 and 1725. It is still in use by the army; as a result, the church, prison, and main guardhouse have resisted the assaults of time. These days it is a much more peaceful enclave than its history would suggest. The walkways, which overlook the moat, are popular with joggers and walkers, and inside there are long, red brick, slate-roofed buildings; a parade ground; a distinguished yellow-painted house dating from 1725; and something unexpected – a windmill from the mid-19th century. The Citadel is open daily from 6 am to 10 pm. Admission is free.

Exit the *Kastellet* through a double archway onto a pathway. This runs over the moat and past a pond, both decorously occupied by swans and coots, and then cuts diagonally away across Churchill Park; in springtime, this park is covered with beds of glorious yellow daffodils. From here, it is worth the effort to stroll along the elegant **Bredgade**, where you will pass the **Museum of Decorative Art** (*Kunstindustrimuseet*). Make a point to stop here at The Café and relax in the *Grønnegården* (see *Museums*, page 67). There are three distinctive churches in this area – **Marble Church** (*Marmorkirken*), **Saint Ansgars Church** (*Sankt Ansgars Kirke*) and the *Alexander Nevsky Kirke*; they are all worth a visit before heading back to Kongens Nytorv. Those with any energy left will want to stroll back to *Rådhuspladsen* by way of the ever-delightful Strøget, others may choose just to hop on a bus (number 6 is one along that route).

Tivoli Gardens

Tivoli, without doubt, is a Copenhagen icon. The concept of public pleasure gardens became popular in European cities during the 18th century. These combine flower gardens and green areas with walking paths, quiet pavilions, restaurants, and stages for music and other forms of entertainment in a lovely ambiance.

In 1843, Georg Carstensen, a widely traveled and quite enterprising man, obtained royal assent to establish a pleasure garden for the citizens of Copenhagen. The design of Carstensen's **Tivoli & Vauxhall Gardens** was based upon one he had seen in Paris. Although Tivoli was built in an area that was, at the time, just outside the city's 19th-century boundaries, over the years Copenhagen has grown; now covering nearly 21 acres, the park provides an oasis of fun and pleasure in a busy 21st-century city.

The gardens have been modernized periodically; new amusements have been introduced and old ones updated, and numerous restaurants have been added. Thankfully, though, these additions and upgrades have been accomplished in a manner that respects the traditional style of the original gardens. The concept remains unchanged, and many time-honored favorites – such as fireworks, performing artists, pantomimes and the world famous **Tivoli Boys**

A considerable number of Danes were upset when the Carlsberg Foundation sold its 43% share of Tivoli Gardens to The Augustinus Foundation, one of Denmark's biggest patrons of the arts, in late 2000.

Guard – date from the garden's early years. Tivoli truly is magic, its ambiance created by both chance and inspiration. There is no single theme to Tivoli. It is exotic, romantic and devised to evoke an atmosphere quite different from day-to-day life. In sum, expect to find the unexpected. It's a reflection of the Danes' desire to enjoy themselves in pleasurable surroundings, a place for all generations to be together and have fun. As such, it is Denmark's most visited attraction, with around four million visitors annually, one-third being non-Danish. This makes it the third most visited amusement park in Europe behind Disneyland Paris and the Blackpool Pleasure Beach in England.

Entertainment at Tivoli abounds; a variety of theaters provides an arena for an impressive diversity of events, from hosting an array of international stars to providing one of the few remaining venues for the ***Commedia dell'Arte*** tradition of pantomime theater. Visitors can get their thrills on any or all of 25 large rides, over half of which are intended for children. The popular roller coaster, the **Turbo Drop**, dates from 1914; it plunges downward from a height of 63 m (206.6 ft) at a speed of 40 mph, exposing those brave enough to try it to a body pressure of 1.5G. The long-time-favorite try-your-strength machine provides an opportunity for buff young lads to impress their lady companions. Evenings are often lit by **fireworks** shows, an institution at Tivoli, and these are produced and manufactured by Tivoli's own pyrotechnists.

TIVOLI is I LOV IT, spelled backwards.

There is no lack of choices for food or drink, with over 38 restaurants (some of gourmet standard) and any number of snack bars, cafés, and beer houses. Alternatively, you can bring a *smørrebrød* (sandwich) from one of the Vesterbrogade shops to a restaurant by the lake, where you may purchase coffee and freely use their plates, cutlery, and napkins.

Surrounding all this entertainment are gardens and green spaces. An average of 400,000 plants will be in bloom at any given time and, after dark, trees and pathways are lit by over 110,000 incandescent lamps whose low intensity produces a soft, warm glow. It is impossible to adequately describe Tivoli in words, as the intent of the pleasure garden is to create a feeling. That it most certainly does, and the feelings evoked here reflect wonderfully Danish priorities – namely to eat, drink and be happy in a peaceful and pleasant ambiance.

CHRISTMAS IN COPENHAGEN

Copenhagen is wonderful enough at any time of the year, but at Christmas it becomes magical, as the Danes' love of life is expressed to the fullest. The season officially begins on December 1st, when all the many Christmas trees in the city are lit up. Tivoli comes alive with a **Christmas Market** that includes small kiosks selling every kind of Christmas merchandise – the small Christmas tree ornaments make wonderful souvenirs. There is also a large hut with several animated Christmas scenes and even an indoor/outdoor train ride. And this is in addition to the garden's usual attractions.

The quayside of the Nyhavn canal is another place to find the holiday spirit; it is lined with small kiosks offering a tantalizing mix of food and gifts. Not to be missed, either, is the circular **ice skating rink** at Kongens Nytorv, where families and friends delight in skating around the equestrian statue of Christian V. Bands playing Christmas tunes can be found everywhere. Seeing the family-oriented Danes delight in all this is a charming, captivating spectacle.

Tivoli is open from mid-April to late September, and the daily program is listed on posters throughout the gardens. General admission is DKK 50, and admission to each entertainment costs between one and four tokens (DKK 10 each). A good option, depending on your plans, may be a one-day pass for DKK 180 that gives unlimited access to entertainments. If you are visiting during the winter, don't miss the famous **Tivoli Christmas Market** that runs from late November until Christmas, offering crafts, gifts, artwork, food and much more. Vesterbrogade 3; ☎ 33-15-10-01 or www.tivoli.dk.

Over 1,600,000 bottles of beer are consumed each year at Tivoli. In other countries, so much free-flowing alcohol would be sure to cause problems, but they are infrequent here and, when someone does get too rumbunctious, the inspectors (Tivoli's own uniformed security guards) take care of the matter swiftly and quietly.

Museums

Fine Arts

DANISH NATIONAL GALLERY
(Statens Museum for Kunst)
Sølvgade 48-50
☎ 33-74-84-94 or www.smk.dk

The Danish National Gallery exhibits nearly 9,000 paintings and sculptures in a light and airy environment. This, Denmark's largest and most prestigious art museum, is housed in two entirely different buildings set in the pleasant **Østre Anlæg** park, which has a large lake full of waterfowl, including some stately gray storks. As visitors approach from the front, the view is of the original classical façade. The thoroughly modern building attached to the rear opened in 1998 after extensive renovations to the museum. This surreal juxtaposition is, nevertheless, a suitable ambiance for the priceless paintings and other art found within. The art here is both Danish and foreign, primarily with origins in western culture, and dates from the 14th century to the present. The collection is particularly strong in 19th-century Danish landscapes and in Dutch and Flemish works from Rembrandt to Paulus Potter. It contains what is perhaps the world's finest collection of Dürer prints. Look, also, for the colorful collection of more modern art. Open year-round on Tuesday, Thursday, Friday, Saturday and Sunday, 10 am to 5 pm; and Wednesday, 10 am to 8 pm. Admission DKK 40.

Copenhagen

NY CARLSBERG GLYPTOTEK
Dantes Plads 7
☎ 33-41-81-41 or www.glyptoteket.dk

This museum is in a distinctive building, dominated by a copper and glass dome, just outside Tivoli Gardens. It is home to of one of the world's foremost collections of Egyptian, Greek, Roman, and Etruscan art – with enough statues and artifacts to equip 100 ancient temples. In complete contrast is the museum's collection of world-class impressionist and post-impressionist art. Works by Gauguin, van Gogh, and Monet, as well as Rodin statues, compete for attention with a complete set of Degas bronzes. This group of 73 delicate statues won the painter posthumous acclaim as a sculptor.

At the Glyptotek, do what the Danes do: take one of the folding stalls that are supplied and sketch your favorite piece of art.

Underneath the dome of the Glyptotek is the **Winter Garden**, an unlikely but nevertheless highly alluring combination of Mediterranean plants set among ponds with goldfish, Roman sarcophagi and contemporary Danish sculpture.

The Glyptotek was founded upon the classical collection of Carl Jacobsen, the Danish brewer and art connoisseur (1842-1914), and then was developed by his family. The museum is open Tuesday through Sunday, 10 am to 4 pm. Admission DKK 30, free on Wednesday and Sunday or with the Copenhagen Card.

THORVALDSEN'S MUSEUM
Porthusgade 2
☎ 33-32-15-32 or www.thorvaldsensmuseum.dk

It is certainly appropriate that one of Copenhagen's most eclectic art collections is housed in this grand and elegant building, which many think of as one of the city's more unusual and atypical. The one-time Royal Coach House, located near Christiansborg Palace, is best viewed from Gammel Strand. From this vantage point you will see an ocher-colored structure that, from the exterior at least, resembles a solid cube. This, though, is deceptive. The interior consists of relatively narrow rooms on two floors; these rooms have beautifully decorated ceilings and enclose a large, very austere patio.

Thorvaldsen's Museum is also his Mausoleum.

In the middle of the patio stands the tomb of **Bertel Thorvaldsen** (1770-1844), considered to be the greatest of Danish sculptors and Copenhagen's only honorary citizen. Returning after 40 years in Rome, Thorvaldsen chose a young architect, Gottlieb Bindesbøll, to design this most unusual museum to house his library and the amazing works in his collection. The Roman and Greek gods and goddesses gazing at you – some mounted on magnificent horses – may seem to be originals, but they are, in fact, 19th-century renditions of antiquity, created by the extraordinary vision of this sculptor. It is noticeable that some of these have turned an ugly gray/black color, the result of air pollution in Rome, where the sculptor had his studio. Thorvaldsen's tomb, though not open for public viewing, is known to be decorated with beautiful patterns.

The museum itself is open Tuesday to Sunday, 10 am to 5 pm. Admission DKK 20, free on Wednesday and with the Copenhagen Card.

THE ROYAL CAST COLLECTION
(*Kongelige Afstøbningssamling*)
Toldbodgade 40
☎ 33-74-84-84

Housed in a beautiful late-18th-century warehouse (*Vestindisk Pakhus*) designed by C.F. Harsdoff, this museum dates from the late 19th century when it – and others like it all over Europe – purchased excellent plaster casts of master works of art from all around the globe, enabling visitors to see representations of famous pieces close at hand. The vast majority of the collection was bought between 1896-1914 by Carl Jacobsen, the brewer turned philanthropist, who made such a lasting impression on his city and who was at that time the director of the museum. Until 1966 the collection was on display at the Statens Museum for Kunst. It was stored in poor conditions for 18 years before being moved here, and it took another 11 years of restoration before the museum could open permanently in 1995. The collection seen today, spread over three floors, is considered one of the best of this type in the world, and these figures from ancient civilizations are fascinating indeed. The museum is open Wednesday and Thursday, 10 am to 4 pm; and Saturday and Sunday, 1 pm to 4:30 pm. Admission DKK 20, or free with the Copenhagen Card.

Casts made from items in the Royal Cast Collection can be exchanged with other for pieces from their collections, or sold to private collectors.

THE HIRSCHSPRUNG COLLECTION
(*Den Hirschsprungske Samling*)
Stockholmsgade 20
☎ 35-42-03-36 or www.hirschsprung.dk

This small, charming museum is in a Greek-inspired neoclassical-style building; the façade is clad in light marble and elaborated with frontons and Doric pilasters. It sits on the opposite side of the Østre Anlæg park from the Danish National Gallery (*Statens Museum for Kunst*). The museum was the brainchild of Heinrich Hirschsprung (1836-1908), of German-Jewish heritage, who arrived in Denmark during the Napoleonic Wars and made his fortune as a cigar manufacturer. His hobby was to collect art from his own period. This collection eventually expanded to include works by the previous generation of painters from the Danish Golden Age. He decided to donate this large collection to the Danish nation in 1902, and was insistent that the collection be given a home of its own with an intimate ambiance not often found in museums of that era. Accordingly, there is a core of large rooms lit from above, surrounded by a series of smaller rooms with windows set high in their walls. In these rooms you will be enchanted by hundreds of examples of Danish art from the 19th century. The artwork is surrounded by contemporary furniture, of which many pieces were donated by the artists themselves. The Hirschsprung Collection is open Thursday to Monday, 11 am to 4 pm; and Wednesday, 11 am to 9 pm. Admission DKK 25, or free with the Copenhagen Card.

DAVID'S ART COLLECTION
(*Davids Samling*)
Kronprinsessegade 30
☎ 33-73-49-49 or www.davidmus.dk

This major collection of Islamic art, along with examples of art and crafts from European countries, was founded by **Christian Ludvig David** (1878-1960), a barrister of the Danish High Court. The collection is housed in a neoclassical building dating from the very early 19th century. Before the fire of 1795 the site belonged to the Rosenborg Have, which is now located just across the road (see page 36).

Open Tuesday and Thursday to Sunday, 1 pm to 4 pm; and Wednesday, 10 am to 4 pm. Admission free.

MUSEUM OF DECORATIVE ART
(*Kunstindustrimuseet*)
Bredgade 68
☎ 33-18-56-56 or www.kunstindustrimuseet.dk

This substantial collection of Danish and European decorative art includes an exhibit of Oriental handicrafts dating from the Middle Ages to the present. The artwork itself may not be to everyone's tastes. The museum, however, is worth a stop simply to enjoy a light meal or homemade baked goods in The Café, with its classic Danish furniture. The Café opens up to the *Grønnegården*, the museum's hidden garden, which is a beautiful green oasis with ivy-covered walls, tree lined avenues, statues and, strangely, seven large urns. The museum and café are open Tuesday to Friday, 10 am to 4 pm; and Saturday and Sunday, noon to 4 pm. Admission DKK 35, or free with Copenhagen Card.

Culture & History

DANISH NATIONAL MUSEUM
(*Nationalmuseet*)
Ny Vestergade 10
☎ 33-13-44-11 or www.natmus.dk

The permanent collections of the National Museum innovatively trace more than 10,000 years of Danish history and culture. This is nothing less than a well-organized labyrinth of artifacts, as diverse as Stone Age rock carvings and Mongolian tents and equestrian equipment. Artifacts here range from prehistoric to modern times, and include, most notably, Egyptian and classical antiquities, coins and medals, and ethnographical and children's displays. Through its colonization of Greenland, Danish culture opens doors on to Eskimo culture, and the exhibition of huskies, igloos, reconstructed Eskimo camps, and medieval clothing from Greenland is well worth a visit as well. Visitors will be intrigued as well by the artifacts that illustrate the prehistoric Denmark that led up to those extraordinary Viking times.

PRINCE'S PALACE

The Danish National Museum is one of the largest museums in Scandinavia. Its main building, the Prince's Palace (*Prinsens Palais*), was originally built in 1684 by a merchant, who sold it to King Frederik IV in 1725. It was rebuilt more than once to serve the royal family, the first time as a residence for crown prince Christian (later King Christian VI). The palace is named after the Margrave (Marquis) Carl of Hessen, who lived in a part of the building in 1766-1767.

The most striking exhibit, though, is a Sun Chariot, dating from 1200 BC. The Danes once worshiped the sun, imagining it just as it is depicted here: a disc of gold riding through the sky in a chariot behind a celestial horse. The museum is open Tuesday to Sunday, 10 am to 5 pm. Admission DKK 40, free on Wednesday and with Copenhagen Card.

MUSEUM EROTICA
Købmagergade 24
☎ 33-12-03-11 or www.museumerotica.dk

Museum Erotica is an unusual museum with unusual opening hours.

Museum Erotica lays claim to being the world's first serious – and seriously – erotic museum. It opened 25 years ago, following the legalization of pornography by the government of Denmark. The collections are prefaced, however, with the disclaimer that they may not be to everyone's tastes.

Although many (if not most) of the museum's collections are inoffensive and interesting, such as some of the special temporary exhibitions, quite a few are nakedly and flagrantly pornographic, and would, most certainly, offend some sensibilities. This applies especially to the bank of multiple TV screens in one gallery, all of which portray colorfully vivid displays of pornography in many of its forms. The museum is open May to September daily from 10 am to 11 pm; at other times of year, it is open daily, 11 am to 8 pm; and Saturday, 10 am to 9 pm. Admission DKK 69.

Military History

DANISH DEFENSE MUSEUM
(*Tøjhusmuseet, Dansk Forsvarsmuseum*)
Tøjhusgade 3
☎ 33-11-60-37

Behind the Royal Stables, in a small side street, resides another museum that is worth a visit just to see the building in which it is housed. It was built by Christian IV between 1598-1604 as an arsenal (*Tøjhus*), and its **Cannon Hall** on the ground floor, at 156 m (511.8 ft) long and 17 m (55.7 ft) wide, is considered to be the world's longest Renaissance hall. The exhibits, which will be of interest to anyone with a penchant for military history, are a fascinating collection of items, from uniforms to airplanes and cannons, some dating from the 15th century. Open Tuesday to Sunday, midday to 4 pm. Admission DKK 30, or free with Copenhagen Card.

MUSEUM OF THE DANISH RESISTANCE
(*Frihedsmuseet*)
Churchillparken
☎ 33-13-77-14 or www.natmus.min.dk

Located, ironically, in one of the prettiest spots in town – especially at daffodil time – is a reminder of grimmer times during the Second World War when many Danes so bravely and stubbornly resisted the German occupying forces. This museum presents a detailed and graphic record of wartime tragedy and of the eventual victory over the Germans. It is open May through mid-September, Tuesday to Saturday, 10 am to 4 pm; and Sunday until 5 pm; at other times of the year it is open Tuesday to Saturday, 11 am to 3 pm; and Sunday until 4 pm. Admission DKK 30, free on Wednesday or with the Copenhagen Card.

ROYAL DANISH NAVAL MUSEUM
(*Orlogsmuseet*)
Overgaden oven Vandet 58
☎ 32-54-63-63

These days the honor of taking care of the Royal Barge is bestowed upon Lumskebugten Café, near Churchill Park.

This is one of the premier museums of its type in the world, and it is particularly proud of its collection of over 300 models and ships dating back over 300 years. The largest of these is a 12-m (39-ft) **royal barge** named the *White Chalouppe* that was in use up to 1918. It is so large that a hole had to be knocked in the wall to get it into the building. This museum, on the banks of the Christianshavn canal, was opened on October 4th, 1989, by Queen Margrethe II. It is housed in the 18th-century *Søkvæsthus* building that, although ideally suited for its current purpose, was originally meant to be a hospital.

At the Naval Museum you will also see a magnificent crowned elephant head, with the letter "D" engraved underneath the tusks; this was part of the figurehead from the ship of the line *Elephanten*, which was launched in 1741 and subsequently sank in the harbor.

The Naval Museum is open Tuesday to Sunday from midday to 4 pm. Admission DKK 30, or free with the Copenhagen Card.

Music History

MUSICAL HISTORY MUSEUM
(*Musikhistorisk Museum*)
Åbenrå 30
☎ 33-11-27-26

Music lovers will definitely be tuned in here. Within three cleverly restored buildings is a collection of European instruments spanning 900 years, and examples of traditional instruments from Europe, Asia and Africa. It is open May to September, daily except Thursday, 1 pm to 3:50 pm; and at other times of the year, Monday, Wednesday, Saturday and Sunday, during the same hours. Admission is DKK 30, or free with the Copenhagen Card.

Churches

Copenhagen, unlike other major cities in Scandinavia, has a wide selection of interesting historic churches; the best of these are described below. Three additional churches, which are also important, are listed in the *Royal Architecture* section (see page 41).

Danish Lutheran

CHURCH OF OUR LADY
(*Vor Frue Kirke*)
Frue Plads
☎ 33-15-10-78 or www.koebenhavnsdomkirke.dk

There has been a church on this site since 1191, when Bishop Absalon appointed his younger relative, Peder Sunesen, Bishop of Roskilde. On July 24th, 1314, the original structure burned down. The new Gothic-style church, completed in 1316, had strong similarities to St. Peter's Church in Malmö, Sweden. The church dominated the city and went on to accumulate great wealth. Vor Frue Kirke was the site of coronation ceremonies from the time of King Christian I in 1448 until the Absolute Monarchy was decreed in 1660.

It is no coincidence that Copenhagen's **University** is adjacent to the cathedral. In 1474, Christian I returned from Rome with a Papal Charter for a university, to be built next to the church; it was inaugurated on June 1st, 1479.

To help recoup the expenses involved in the restoration, a carillon was installed at Vor Frue Kirke in 1746 and a fee was charged for the use of the bells at funerals, weddings and christenings!

The initial waves of the Reformation brought with them, on December 30th, 1530, an invasion of the church by a crowd of distinguished citizens, who tore down altars and images of saints. Later, in October 1536, the old bishopric was dissolved and new bishops were appointed. The 14th century Gothic structure was destroyed by the Great Fire of 1728, only to be rebuilt on a grander scale. When it was completed in 1738, after six years of construction, it was the largest cathedral in the country. Its spire, completed in 1744, was the tallest of Copenhagen's towers at 120 m (384 ft).

Once more, this time as the result of the British bombardment of Copenhagen on September 2nd, 1807, the church was destroyed by fire; the Crown

Prince, later to be Frederik VI, designated an architect, C.F. Hansen, who had a definite preference for the neoclassical style of architecture, to design a new church. The plans were approved by the king on June 4th, 1811, but construction proceeded slowly due to the extreme poverty of the country. As a consequence, it was not until June 7th, 1829, that the new church was consecrated. To create a grand impression in the large, austere interior, King Frederik VI turned to sculptor Bertel Thorvaldsen (see page 66), who had returned to Copenhagen from Rome in 1819. The artist created an impressive collection of massive statues depicting Christ and the 12 Apostles.

Vor Frue Kirke is open May 1st to September 30th, Monday, Tuesday, Wednesday, Thursday and Saturday from 8:30 am to 4:30 pm; Friday, 8:30 am to 10:30 am, and midday to 4:30 pm; and Sunday, midday to 4:30 pm. The rest of the year it is open the same hours, except on Sunday, when it opens from midday to 1 pm, and 3 pm to 4:30 pm. Admission is free.

CHURCH OF THE HOLY GHOST
(*Helligåndskirken*)
Niels Hemmingsens Gade 5
☎ 33-15-41-4

The history of this church goes as far back as 1296, when it was part of a monastery of the same name. In fact, the entrance from the church close, the *Helligåndshuset*, is the original west wing of the monastery, and is the only completely preserved medieval structure in Copenhagen.

The monastery was famed for its charitable spirit, and it received papal recognition when King Christian I visited Rome in 1474. Although the monastery was disbanded in 1536, during the Reformation, the building did receive a new lease on life as a parish church. However, it was not so lucky in 1728 when it was destroyed by the Great Fire. Some adjacent structures were spared, and the church was rebuilt by 1732, but most of what you see today dates from a major restoration at the end of the 19th century. Open Monday to Friday from midday to 4 pm.

CHRISTIAN'S CHURCH
(*Christians Kirke*)
Strandgade 1
☎ 32-96-83-01

At the turn of the 18th century, Christianshavn was home to many foreigners, particularly Germans. It was they who, in 1749, requested from King Frederik V the right to construct their own place of worship. Permission was granted, and Nicolai Eigtved (the architect and town planner responsible for the *Marmorkirken*, Royal Theater and much other development during this era) was commissioned to design a church. It was consecrated in 1759; its steeple, which now dominates the immediate area, was completed a decade later. Known as **Frederik's German Church**, it served its purpose until the late 19th century, when it was reconsecrated as a Danish parish church and given its present name. The rococo interior is unusual in that it resembles a theater; taking advantage of that fact this church, unlike other Danish Lutheran-evangelical ones, holds activities that include rock and ballet concerts. In the crypt there are 48 sepulchral chapels separated by elegant wrought-iron latticework. Open daily, 8 am to 5 pm.

MARBLE CHURCH
(*Marmorkirken*)
Frederiksgade 4
☎ 33-15-01-44

This area of Copenhagen was very fashionable in the early 18th century. In 1740, King Frederik V commissioned the town planner and architect, Nicolai Eigyved, to create a monument to honor the 300th anniversary of the House of Oldenburg. Eigyved designed a church to be built of marble, surrounded by statues of important people from Danish and Christian history. King Frederik laid the foundation stone in October 1749, but the increasingly prohibitive cost of the Norwegian marble specified for the building forced the prime minister, Struensee, to halt construction in 1770; for more than a century the church remained a picturesque ruin. In 1874 the financier C.F. Tietgen purchased the plot and, at his own expense (and supplementing the Norwegian marble with marble from Faxe in Denmark), finished the construction. The church was consecrated on August 19, 1894 as an Evangelical Lutheran Church of Denmark.

The majestic dome is one of the largest church domes in Europe at a full 31 m (100 ft) in diameter. Approaching the building you will note that, at ground level and on the roof terrace, the church is surrounded by many statues. At the lower level these represent famous persons from Danish Church history, including St. Ansgar, who helped bring the Christian religion to Denmark; and Grundtvig, a 19th-century educationalist. Above these are additional statues of 16 important figures from international Christian history, ranging from Moses to Luther. The dome is supported by 12 formidable pillars, each decorated with rich frescoes in blue, gold, and green, representing Christ's Apostles. Inside,

Marble Church is also known as Frederiks Church (Frederiks Kirke).

the church is impressively beautiful, but only the lower levels are of marble.

Marble Church is open Monday, Tuesday, Thursday, Friday and Saturday, 10:30 am to 4:40 pm; Wednesday, 10:30 am to 6 pm; and Sunday, midday to 4:30 pm. Guided tours of the dome are conducted daily from mid-June through August, at 1 pm and 3 pm; and the rest of the year on Saturday and Sunday, 1 pm and 3 pm.

TRINITY CHURCH
Trinitatis Kirke)
Landemærket 2
☎ 33-12-91-80

Trinity was constructed in the mid-17th century, at the same time as the adjacent Round Tower, for the benefit of students of the university. The foundation stone was laid in 1637 and construction was completed in 1656. A year later, in 1657, the University Library of Copenhagen was installed in the loft above the church. This, though, proved an unfortunate choice; the Great Fire of 1728 destroyed the library along with most of the church. What you see is a reconstruction, in Northern Gothic-baroque style, dating from the years following the fire. These days the church is famous for its **Chamber Choir** (*Trinitatis Kantori*), which was formed in 1993. Trinity Church is open 9:30 am to 4:30 pm, daily.

Anglican

ST. ALBANS ANGLICAN EPISCOPAL CHURCH
(*St. Albans Engeske Kirke*)
Churchillparken
☎ 33-11-85-18 or www.st-albans.dk

In Churchill Park, the most unlikely looking outline of a church appears. Unlikely, because it looks nothing at all like any other church you will see in Copenhagen; indeed, this classically Victorian Gothic structure would look much more at home in an English country village. It owes its existence to its royal connections; the Prince of Wales, later to become King Edward VII of England, was married to Princess Alexandra of Denmark. She decided that the British congregation in Copenhagen should have their own church. Construction began in 1885. When the church was consecrated in 1897 it was one of the first foreign denominations to be granted royal approval to hold services – a privilege previously restricted to the Danish Folk Church (*den danske folkekirke*, an earlier name for the Danish National Church). The British connection is still strong as the church is actually under the patronage of HM Queen Elizabeth II. St. Albans is only open for services.

Roman Catholic

SAINT ANSGARS CHURCH
(*Sankt Ansgars Kirke*)
Bredgade 64
☎ 33-13-37-62

Construction of St. Ansgars was funded by a legacy from Peter Bianco, a wine merchant; it was built between 1840 and 1842, and originally served as a private chapel for the Austrian Embassy. In 1865, in honor of the 1,000th anniversary of the death of the Benedictine monk Ansgar, it was reconsecrated and renamed. St. Ansgars now serves Copenhagen's modest Roman Catholic community.

The bell tower was added in 1943, and in 1953 the church was elevated to the status of cathedral. Between 1988 and 1992 it underwent a major restoration. The ornate interior departs from Catholic tradition. It is decorated with paintings by the German, Josef Settegast, and has fixtures and fittings in the

French Empire style. A small museum within the church documents the history of Catholicism in the city since its near extinction in the Reformation of 1536. Saint Ansgars is open daily, 8 am to 6 pm.

Ansgar was popularly known as The Nordic Apostle.

Russian Orthodox

ALEXANDER NEVSKY KIRKE
Bredgade 53

This church, built for Copenhagen's Russian Orthodox community between 1881 and 1883, is immediately recognizable by its three golden onion-shaped cupolas; it is very much out of context on this busy street. Open, of course, during services, and also on Tuesday, Wednesday and Thursday, 11:30 am to 1:30 pm.

Public Parks

It is surprising that a city as small as Copenhagen is so well endowed with parks and green spaces – that is, until you realize that many of these open areas were once parts of the defensive fortifications of the city.

BOTANICAL GARDENS
(*Botanisk Have*)
Gothersgade 128
☎ 33-32-22-22 or www.botanic-garden.ku.dk

Although, at 10 hectares (24.7 acres), this is not the largest open green area in Copenhagen, it is certainly the most attractive. Founded in 1872 along Copenhagen's old city walls, this is the fourth botanical garden belonging to the university to be established in Copenhagen since 1600. The old fortifications and ramparts give the gardens an undulating structure; the moat has been transformed into a beautiful lake. Within this environment, charming even to non-plant lovers, is Denmark's largest collection of living plants – approximately 25,000 specimens from more than 13,000 species. Not to be missed, either, are the garden's amazing greenhouses. These were originally constructed in the 1870s and were extensively renovated just over a century later. The most prominent of these is the impressive **Palm House**, which has a metal spiral stairway leading to a walkway around the second level. The gardens are open 8:30 am to 6 pm, in summer; there is no admission fee.

ØSTRE ANLÆG

The Botanical Gardens are bounded on both sides by two more parks; these were also part of the city's fortifications. Østre Anlæg, the closer of the two, is across the road; it was originally laid out in the form of an English garden in 1871, making it marginally the older. Here, too, the moat has been transformed into an attractive lake that is home to a wide variety of waterfowl and other birds. There are numerous statues and monuments as well as pleasant flowerbeds throughout the garden. Within the park, at the end closest to the Botanical Gardens, are two museums: the **Statens Museum for Kunst** and the **Hirschsprung Collection** (see *Museums*, pages 62 and 65).

H. C. ØRSTEDSPARKEN

Just three blocks away on the other side of the Botanical Gardens is the smaller, but no less attractive, H.C. Ørstedsparken. It is named after, and contains a statue of, the famous Danish physicist H.C. Ørsted, who is credited with discovering electromagnetism. This park was also laid out in the English style; it dates from 1876 to 1879. Although it is not well known to visitors, it is highly popular with the locals. Open May 1 to September 30 daily,

8:30 am to 6 pm; and October 1 to April 30 on Tuesday to Sunday, 8:30 am to 4 pm. The main greenhouse opens daily from 10 am to 3 pm. The other, smaller ones have varying opening schedules.

KING'S GARDEN
(*Kongens Have*)
Øster Voldgade 4b
☎ 33-13-47-65

Just across the busy Øster Voldgade from the Botanical Gardens is this park; it is the most visited in Copenhagen, drawing crowds of over 2.5 million annually. In fact, these are the oldest royal gardens in Denmark, having been landscaped simultaneously with the construction of the adjacent **Rosenborg Castle** (see page 36), which was completed in 1624. The park was originally laid out in the Renaissance style, with a characteristically rectangular network of pathways that largely exists to this day, despite changes in fashion – from Renaissance to baroque to romantic – through the 17th, 18th and 19th centuries. The King's Garden is adorned with many sculptures and fountains. The neoclassical **Hercules Pavilion**, the third one on the site, now houses a café; this is particularly pleasant in the warmer months when you can sit outside. Since 1996 the **Green Bridge**, *Grønnebro*, has allowed visitors to walk directly from Rosenborg Castle to the gardens, a privilege once reserved for kings. In one corner of the park, between the palace and Gothersgade, visitors today will see a large parade ground for the use of the **Queen's Guards**. It is here that the troops muster for the changing of the guard at Amelienborg. In the early 18th century this was laid out as a parterre by King Frederik IV's landscape architect. Note, also, that many of the little guard houses next to the park's gates have been transformed into specialty and craft stores, among other things. On national holidays you are likely to see large family groups, having staked out their own areas with miniature Danish flags, enjoying copious amounts of beer and other beverages, as well as mountains of food. Often the oldest member of the family will be seated in the middle of the group on a favorite chair.

The park is open daily, year-round. Hours vary, with opening time generally at 7 am and closing time between 5 and 10 pm, depending on the season. Admission is free.

FREDERIKSBERG HAVE & ZOOLOGISK HAVE

This garden, which surrounds the large **Frederiksberg Castle**, is in the western section of the city, directly behind the **Copenhagen Zoo**. Its symmetrical plan, supposedly inspired by gardens visited on one of King Frederik IV's trips to Italy, was laid out at the beginning of the 17th century in the baroque style. Fashions changed in the following century, and the garden was transformed into the English country style, which is what you will find today. It is a very open park, with ponds connected by a network of canals. One of its most inviting features is the abundance of bird life, some of which is from the zoo next door. Of interest, too, is the Chinese Pavilion that sits right next to the exit from the garden to the zoo; unfortunately, these days, it is rather run down.

Visitors to the castle and zoo can take the S-Train to Valby, or bus numbers 6, 18, 28, 39, 100S, 171E, 172E or 550S.

Day-Trips

Amager

The island of Amager is located across the harbor from Copenhagen. Sunday is a good day to hop on a number 30 bus from Rådhuspladsen and venture out to the small seafaring towns of **Store Magleby** and **Dragør**. Not only is Dragør charming in its own right, it also boasts a goodly number of eclectic specialty stores that are open on Sundays when many shops in Copenhagen are closed.

AMAGER MUSEUM
(*Amagermuseet*)
Hovedgaden 4 & 12
Store Magleby
☎ 32-53-02-50

This short trip is best taken during the summer months.

Your first stop is the village of **Store Magleby**. Here, in an old farmhouse on the village's main street, you will find a museum that will go some way to explain the unusual history of this coastal area. The museum is actually a home laid out in the traditional style, complete with furnished bedrooms and kitchen. Beginning in 1901 the collection was donated by villagers from the surrounding area who wanted to present, in a straightforward manner, the reasons for the area's prevailing Dutch atmosphere. King Christian II, who reigned from 1513 to 1523, invited a colony of farmers from the Netherlands to come and improve soil cultivation in the area, in order to provide the royal table with "as many roots and onions as are needed." He granted these Dutch immigrants special privileges to live in Store Magleby, which for centuries was referred to as *Hollænderbyen* (Dutchmen's Town). They had their own judicial system and church (with services in Dutch or Low German only), and developed a unique local costume derived from a combination of Dutch, Danish, and French styles. A large collection of examples of this traditional costume is on display at the museum. It is open May to September, Tuesday to Sunday, midday to 4 pm; and at other times of the year on Wednesday and Sunday during the same hours. Admission DKK 20, or free with Copenhagen Card.

DRAGØR

After visiting the museum and the town, reboard the number 30 bus for the remaining 2½ km (1½ mile) trip to Dragør. The town was built on a promontory on the Øresund between Zealand and Sweden. This strategic location made it a natural landing point for those crossing between Denmark and **Scania** (*Skåne*). The most southern of Sweden's provinces, its ownership has passed from Sweden to Denmark and back at different times in its history. The strait was blessed with an abundance of fish, particularly herring. From the mid-14th century, when Dragør was granted royal trading privileges, until the early 16th century, the town was an important player in the Scania markets. Traders came to these markets from far and wide. Between July and October they purchased and traded for the pickled herring that was, at that time, a much-favored food in Catholic Europe. During the remaining non-market months of the year, Dragør was depopulated. It wasn't until nearly the end of that era that a permanent settlement was founded on this site. It was around this time that the Dutch began to settle at Store Magleby. Dragør subsequently came under the control of the Dutch settlers and remained so until 1822. In fact, it was the Dutch who built the harbor at Dragør and, during the late 17th century, the population of Dragør grew dramatically. An influx of farmers moved to Dragør from Store Magleby as the population of the latter village began to outgrow the available farmland. At the same time, immigrants came from Scania after it was ceded to Sweden in 1658. Throughout most of the 17th and 18th centuries, prosperity continued as the fleet grew. By the late 1770s, however, the decline of the fishing industry brought about a concurrent downturn in Dragør's fortunes; despite a brief revival in the late 1800s, the town's influence as a maritime presence was over by the end of the 19th century. These days, visitors will find an absolutely enchanting experience here. The harbor is chock-full of small boats, and the 18th-century village remains remarkably preserved. A maze of cobbled streets and alleyways leads off from a single traffic road, and a stroll between the charming half-timbered, thatched or tile-roofed cottages with their postage-stamp gardens gives a vivid impression of what life was like in earlier times.

Next to the harbor in Dragør, on the Havnepladsen, is the oldest house in the town, a circa-1682 fisherman's cottage, which has been imaginatively converted into the **Dragør Museum**. This museum, devoted to local seafaring history, is open from May through September, Tuesday to Friday, 2 to 5 pm; and Saturday and Sunday, midday to 6 pm.

The **Mølstead Museum**, at Dr. Dichs Plads 1 in the center of Dragør, is also worth a visit. Christian Mølstead (1862 to 1930) specialized in paintings with marine and local themes, and many of his works are displayed here. Opening hours are May to August, Saturday and Sunday, 2 to 5 pm. The phone number for either of these museums is ☎ 32-53-41-06; the combined entrance fee is DKK 20, or free with the Copenhagen card.

From Dragør, you can catch the bus back to Rådhuspladsen. But, while you're here, why not treat yourselves to lunch at the harbor-front **Dragør Strandhotel**, ☎ 32-53-00-75. This establishment, which dates back more than 700 years, is one of Denmark's oldest; it is a place where you can combine history and fine cuisine – especially from their menu of delicious fish dishes.

Humlebæk

Some people may question why, with so many fine museums in the city itself, they should undertake this trip to a town about 45 minutes by train from Copenhagen, and just south of Helsingør (see below). Well, for a start, there is the Louisiana Museum's outstanding collection of international and Danish art, in the form of paintings, drawings and graphic art and sculptures from the 20th century. The architecture and the setting of the museum are just as much of an attraction.

LOUISIANA MUSEUM OF MODERN ART
Gl. Strandvej 13
Humlebæk
☎ 49-19-07-19 (information) or ☎ 49-19-07-20 (for tickets), www.louisiana.dk

The museum has grown around a tasteful villa on 25 acres of land undulating gently toward the banks of the Øresund. The property was made over to the Master of the Royal Hunt, **Alexander Brun**, in 1855. Brun himself was an interesting man. He was well known for his progressive methods of fruit growing and bee-keeping; in fact he inserted a clause in his will to the effect that any person who so wished could demand a shoot from one of the apple or pear trees in the orchard. Although a portion of the orchards had to make way for the south wing, the museum still retains this caveat and, theoretically at least, on presentation of an admission ticket a visitor can demand a shoot from one of the fruit trees.

Alexander Brun's unusual personal life was responsible for the name of the villa; he was married three times, and each of his wives was named Louise!

Entrance to the Louisiana is through the original white-walled mansion; it was here that exhibits were first opened to the public in 1958. At that time the concept of establishing an interplay between visual art, architecture and landscape was new. In those days, the Louisiana was exclusively a collection of modern Danish art. Since then it has grown to include international works. Expansion was soon necessary, and two wings were added. The design of the additions placed special emphasis on the effects of natural light from above. The new layout, however, required visitors either to retrace their steps or to walk through the park to reach the separate parts of the museum. Later additions alleviated this inconvenience. They were built into the sloping terrain of the park, making them more or less invisible, and they allow visitors to walk the whole way around the museum, albeit on different levels.

In addition to the permanent collections, the Louisiana Museum of Modern Art holds six to eight major exhibitions of contemporary art from around the world, including the works of new and upcoming artists as well as that of the modern masters. Unlike some museums, the Louisiana places an emphasis on sculpture, to the point that the museum's park can be considered a romantic garden with sculptures. To encapsulate, it can be said that the Louisiana Museum of Modern Art is a combination of modernity and good taste.

The town of Humlebæk is 35 km (about 22 miles) north of Copenhagen; it is best reached by train from Central Station, on S-Tog's Helsingør line. As you exit the station, make a left turn at the main road and follow that until you see the signs for the museum; it's a walk of about 10 to 15 minutes. This is at the very least a half-day trip, and most visitors will want to take their time and enjoy this unusual ambiance at a leisurely pace. With that in mind, why not plan a lunch at the pleasing **Museum Café**, from which you have beautiful views of both the Sculpture Park and Øresund. The Louisiana is open daily, 10 am to 5 pm; on Wednesday, 10 am to 10 pm. Admission DKK 68, higher for special exhibitions.

With Helsingør being so close, just a short bus (number 358 from outside the Louisiana) or train trip, some might be tempted to combine both places on a single day-trip; this, though, would not permit you to see either at its best.

Shop Till You Drop

Shopping Center

FISKETORVET
Kalvebod Brygge 59

So called because it is built on the site of a former fish market, Fisketorvet is next to a canal just a short bus or waterbus trip away from the city center. Only recently opened, it has over 100 stores, 15 restaurants and 10 cinemas, making it the largest shopping center in Denmark. In a typically European manner, it is anchored by two hypermarkets (a combination of a department store and supermarket), **Føtex** and **Kvickly**, that open an hour earlier than the other shops. Although most of the stores are of Scandinavian origin, the market does have a small international presence. Open Monday to Friday, 10 am to 8 pm; and Saturday, 9 am to 5 pm. Reached by bus number 150S from Rådhuspladsen, or the DFDS Water Bus Blue Tour (see page 25).

The shops in Fisketorvet have the longest opening hours in Copenhagen.

Shopping Streets

Strøget

Among Copenhagen's many claims to fame is that, since 1962 (when **Østergade** was closed to vehicles), it has been home to the world's longest pedestrian-only shopping street. It starts near **Rådhuspladsen** and winds its way for about a kilometer (¾ mile), arriving finally at the impressive **Kongens**

Nytorv square. Strøget is quite a mixed bag these days, playing host to street markets, numerous small bars, restaurants, cafés and, often, a variety of street performers trying to part you from a few kroner. It has an amazingly eclectic array of stores, ranging from tacky tourist shops to high-end, and expensive, specialty stores. Above all, you can be assured that, day or night, this traffic-free haven is never boring. Be sure to allocate some time to explore the side streets running off Strøget, where you'll find more surprises among the antique shops, boutiques and fashionable restaurants.

SHOPPING TIPS

There are simply so many shopping experiences to be had in Copenhagen that not only is it next to impossible to find them all, but it is certainly impossible to detail them here. There is help at hand, though, in the form of a booklet titled *Funshopping København*; it costs DKK 40, and is fairly easily found at places of business in Copenhagen. Illustrated, informative and with shops cross-referenced back to city plans, this is a must for serious shoppers.

Strædet

Strædet is approximately parallel to, and a close cousin of, Strøget, but a lot less busy and commercial. It is made up of two streets, **Læderstræde** and **Kompagnestræde**. It is along here, and on the streets leading to and from Strøget, that you will find the majority of antique and specialty stores in Copenhagen.

Department Store

MAGASIN DU NORD
Vingårdstræde 6
☎ 33-11-44-33

Every country in Europe has its own famous department store, and Denmark is not an exception. This one was the inspiration of two friends, Theodor Wessel and Emil Vett, who opened their first store, Emil Vett & Co., in 1868 at Århus. Obviously, they had to have a presence in the capital, so in 1870 they opened a branch in the Hotel du Nord, which had an impressive façade opening on to Kongens Nytorv; within a decade the name had been changed to reflect its location. By the beginning of the 20th century there were 98 stores in the chain, but by the 1950s the company's strategy had been modified; the new focus was on fewer, but much larger, stores. In 1994 the parent company, A/S Th. Wessel & Vett, consolidated its position in the marketplace by purchasing 100% of Illum, a competitor that had opened its first store in 1891. These days it has just seven other Magasin department stores; these are in Lyngby, Rødovre, Odense, Kolding, Aalborg, Århus and a store called **City 2** in Taastrup, as well as the **Illum** store on Amagertorv Square (see page 53).

To meet the demands of the new millennium, Wessel & Vett developed a new marketing strategy. Magasin has retained its status as a department store, but the new core target group is families with two children living at home. Illum has become a lifestyle center, with individual retailers selling their own products under the umbrella of the New Illum name, which is administered by the parent company.

Magasin du Nord's Copenhagen store is truly impressive; it is directly accessible from the new Metro stop at Kongens Nytorv. Serious shoppers will want to pay special attention to the specialized department of gastronomy, which appears as a large kitchen with specially trained staff. The main attraction here is the vast array of semi-professional kitchen tools and appliances, many of which are not readily available outside Denmark. Check out, too, the attractive array of papers and pens in the ground floor stationery department.

Browsers will enjoy the experience of simply visiting the store, and no one will want to leave Magasin du Nord without investigating the famous **Mad & Vin** (Food and Wine) section that – as well as being a gastronomic paradise – offers demonstrations by visiting chefs and food journalists.

The management at Magasin du Nord wants to make your visit a truly fulfilling experience; to achieve this, you shouldn't leave without stopping for a bite to eat and a refreshing drink at one of the very attractive and innovative cafés and bars spread throughout the store. And, to show that they are really up-to-date in their thinking, they have provided a small Internet area for shoppers, with very reasonable hourly rates. Magasin is open Monday to Thursday, 10 am to 7 pm; Friday, 10 am to 8 pm; and Saturday, 10 am to 5 pm.

Specialty Stores

Cigars, Cigarettes & Tobacco

W.Ø. LARSEN
Amagertorv 9

This shop has been in business for over 400 years. It is a "must" for those desiring to purchase Cuban, or other, cigars, as well as any of its numerous varieties of tobacco and its wide array of cigarettes. These products are interesting enough in their own right. But even if you are not a smoker the shop is worth a visit; in the basement you will find a museum that claims to have Europe's most beautiful collection of tobacco-related antiquities.

Clothing

HELLY HANSEN SHOPPEN
Nøregade 47
☎ 33-12-20-58

No matter what season you visit Denmark, but especially in the winter months, you are likely to need windproof and waterproof clothing, and no brand offers you a better selection than Helly Hansen. In business since the late 19th century, they now offer a complete range of stylish jackets, shoes and socks, underwear, sweaters, mittens and even sunglasses. In the cold months, you will see Danish children walking around in jumpsuits, which cover them from head to toe. Helly Hansen has a great selection of these, and they make great gifts for your children back at home.

IXTLAN
Larsbjørnsstræde 19
☎ 33-11-33-81

This rather small store has an amazing array of handicrafts, all of which have been personally selected by its gregarious owner. Colorful and interesting, these include such things as glass, ceramics, baskets, candleholders, wooden animals, textiles, bags, toys and even South American hammocks. The most discerning shoppers, though, will ask to see the very fine collection of Oleana knitwear from Norway. Made in a small factory in Bergen, these are extremely beautiful products. The full range includes skirts, jewelry and even wrist warmers – practical as well as fashionable.

If you are looking for a really special, and unusual, gift for a woman in your life then knitwear from Ixtlan is certainly it.

THE SWEATER MARKET
Frederiksberggade 15
☎ 33-15-27-73
www.sweatermarket.com

While sweaters, especially Norwegian ones, are sold in many places, The Sweater Market claims to be Europe's largest store of its kind; it always has at least 8,000 sweaters in stock on its two floors, plus all manner of accessories such as mittens, scarves, socks and caps.

Dale of Norway is considered one of the best brands of knitwear. More about that company, their range of products, and a listing of merchants can be found at www.dale.no.

Down Comforters

OFELIA
Amagertorv 3
☎ 33-12-41-98

This store specializes in the finest goosedown comforters, and the charming proprietors will delight in explaining to you the finer points of their products. You will learn that down, which comes from the chest of a goose, is rounded and flexible with loose fibers; its construction allows air to circulate, providing excellent insulation (it should come as no surprise that geese from northern climates produce the best down). On the other hand, feathers are flat and the fibers are tightly arranged This tends to restrict the flow of air between them, so that they insulate much less effectively. Feathers are also brittle and, being prone to breakage, do not withstand wear as well as down. Consequently, the higher the percentage of down, with the maximum available being 95%, the better the quality of a comforter.

Quality, which relates to the percentage of actual down as opposed to feathers, is important, and will determine how long the comforter retains its as-purchased condition.

EIDERDOWN

Many readers, especially those middle-aged or older, will be familiar with the term *eiderdown*. This author, who grew up in the UK in the days before central heating, certainly is. What he didn't know, and most readers may not either, is that this brown-colored down comes from the **Eider duck** that is raised in special habitats, generally in Iceland and Greenland. Because this down is scarcer and more difficult to extract, comforters made with eiderdown are significantly more expensive.

Ofelia makes comforters in five different thicknesses, with the decision as to which level of thickness to purchase determined by both personal preference and climate. That said, it could be a real problem for couples when one prefers it colder, or warmer, than the other. Ofelia has a solution for this – buy a separate comforter for each side of the bed: a thicker one for the cold-natured person and a thinner one for the hot-natured one. You will want, also, to take a look at Ofelia's range of quality comforter covers. These are functional and decorative, as they protect the comforter from soiling. Before leaving Ofelia's, be sure to check out their interesting accessories – such as the unusual down slippers, which are ideal for keeping your toes toasty while sitting around watching TV or surfing the Internet.

Fine Housewares

ROYAL COPENHAGEN PORCELAIN
Amagertorv 6
☎ 33-13-71-81
www.royalshopping.com

For most people the name Royal Copenhagen, a company that celebrated its 225th anniversary in 2000, is synonymous with fine porcelain. It is quite appropriate, then, that the beautiful façade of number 6, a Renaissance house dating from 1616, is home to Royal Copenhagen Porcelain. There, on three floors, you can view the largest collection of Royal Copenhagen porcelain in the world, including the famous Flora Danica dinner service pattern.

The showroom is open Monday to Thursday, 10 am to 6 pm; Friday, 10 am to 7 pm; Saturday, 10 am to 5 pm; and in some locations on Sunday, in summer only, midday to 5 pm.

If you are a serious shopper looking for a bargain, plan to take a guided tour of the Royal Scandinavia Porcelain Manufactory in the suburb of Frederiksberg; this is easily reached by bus #1 from the Central Station area toward Rodovre, or bus #14 from the Town Square toward Vanlose. The tours, lasting about one hour, begin with a video presentation. This is followed by visits to the museum, showroom, and workshop, where you will see, first hand, how these skilled artisans create the famous Royal Copenhagen patterns on this delicate porcelain. Tours are offered in Danish and English, and take place Monday to Friday, at 9 am, 10 am, 11 am, 1 pm and 2 pm; the cost is DKK 25 per person. They end at the Factory Shop, which sells a wide selection of "seconds" at very favorable prices. If you wish to forego the tour and simply hunt for bargains, the Factory Shop is open for business Monday to Friday, 9 am to

5:30 pm; and Saturday, 9 am to 2 pm. The factory is located at Smallegade 47; ☎ 38-86-48-59.

SKANDINAVISK GLAS
Ny Østergade 4 (just off Strøget)
☎ 33-13-80-95
Fax 33-32-33-35
www.skandinavskglas.com

There are numerous stores that sell crystal and porcelain in Copenhagen, but there are special reasons for heading toward the glittering displays found here. Not only does this shop carry all of the well-known Scandinavian brands, such as Royal Copenhagen, Orrefors, Kosta Boda and Mats Jonasson, it also offers the widest selection from other major European companies – Baccarat, Herend, Hummel, and Lladró to name a few.

SHOP BY MAIL

For those who delight in collecting these beautiful pieces, Skandinavisk Glas has a mail order brochure, sent out in spring and fall; it includes a complete list of old Danish Christmas plates from both Royal Copenhagen and Bing & Grøndhal (prices listed in US$ include the shipping cost). To get on this list you can call or fax the numbers listed above, or check out their website for an e-mail link.

ZWILLING J.A. HENCKELS A/S
Vimmelskaftet 47 (just across from Jorcks Passage)
☎ 33-12-66-77

For those sharp enough to know, the Zwilling J.A. Henckels name has been famous since 1731 for their superb collection of high quality knives, scissors and tableware. In those early days, their customers were royalty, artisans and merchants; but today the complete range of Zwilling products is readily available to everyone. This store also carries a unique selection of Norwegian pewter and an impressive collection of cocktail, bar, kitchen and cooking utensils, many of which are not easily found in North America.

Food & Drink

A.C. PERCH'S THEHANDEL
Kronprinsensgade 5.
☎ 33-15-35-62
www.perchs-the.dk

Dating from 1835, this is a lovely, old-fashioned shop with a most attractive interior. It is operated by the fourth generation of the Hincheldey family, proprietors since 1894. Its specialty is loose tea, with samples of every imaginable variety imported from the best plantations in the world. Without doubt, even the most discriminating connoisseur of this most civilized of brews will find something here to appeal. Of course, proper brewing of the tea demands a teapot, and there is a fine choice here, along with attractive storage tins and even marmalade for the scones!

OLE JENSEN APS
Købmagergade 32 (just off Strøget)
☎ 33-12-94-03

Cheese lovers will adore this mouthwateringly enticing store; it has on display over 300 varieties, including strong Danish ones and many international selections. Of course, to accompany the cheese there are breads and crackers, as well as all kinds of meats and sausages that can be made into take-away sandwiches. This is the place to go if you are partial to a little late-night snack back at your hotel. To complement your selections, choose a vintage from the superior selection of wines. For those planning a trip to

Helsingør (page 147) there is a branch of Ole Jensen Aps at Stengade 19, the main pedestrian shopping street in that town.

Jewelry

HALBERSTADT
Østergade 4
☎ 33-15-97-90 or 33-13-00-97

Amber is indigenous to the Baltic Sea, which, some 60 million years ago, was covered by a dense forest of *pinus succinifera*. Specimens of Baltic amber, which range in age from 55 million to 35 million years old, are comprised of the fossilized resin of this now extinct tree. Amber is found in a variety of colors, from milky white to a rich translucent brown. Jewelry made from amber is unusual in that it contains the remains of insects; once enticed by the sweet scent of the pine resin, they have been trapped forever in the sticky substance.

THE JEWEL IN THE CROWN

This is not, as you might think, a reference to amber jewelry. Rather, the accolade belongs to a diminutive electric train in the Halberstadt store window near the end of Strøget. It runs during business hours around a 41-foot track, drawing the attention of admiring onlookers. The bodies of the 2¼-inch engine and 1¼-inch wagons are made of 18-carat yellow gold; the engine is set with 190 diamonds; and the wagons, which carry cargos of rubies, emeralds, diamonds and sapphires respectively, are set with eight diamonds each. This train has been featured on nearly every major news show throughout the world, and, if you fancy one yourself, has been on offer (for $100,000) in the Nieman Marcus catalogue since 1992.

Violent winter storms cause such turbulence in the Baltic Sea that amber is uprooted from the seabed and washed ashore. The prime locations for collecting amber have been kept secret from generation to generation. The Vikings, in their adventures around the world, traded amber for other goods and thus, early on, it found its way to places far from Denmark. In Greek mythology amber was considered to be the "Tears of the Gods"; Egyptians considered it talismanic; and the Romans wore spectacular amber decorations in parades celebrating their successful military campaigns.

Naturally, there are a number of stores in Copenhagen selling amber, but none can compare, here or anywhere else, to that found at Halberstadt, a family company that has been in business at the same location since 1846. Halberstadt takes pride in its international reputation as the "Connoisseurs of Amber," using only the very finest amber, distinguishable by its absolute smoothness. They are believed to have been the first craftsmen to set amber into a gold frame.

Halberstadt has a department in Fortnum & Mason in London. They trade no one else's jewelry, and every piece on sale is absolutely unique. It is not surprising, then, that the client list includes kings and queens, Danish aristocrats and other famous people from all over the world. They come here for rings, pendants, brooches, bracelets and necklaces that range in price from $50 to $10,000 (more for custom designs). This author's suggestion is to go one step further and consider the jewelry made from green amber, which is particularly unusual and actually changes its color under strobe lighting.

REESLEV
Nygade 6
☎ 33-14-40-68

Found in one of the most prestigious locations in the Nygade section of Strøget, this store is an experience in itself even if you are only window-shopping. However, it is much more interesting to pass the two model guards at the front door and meet the young, but nevertheless experienced, highly innovative and very friendly proprietors, Torben Hansen, his girlfriend Stella Tesilanu (a Moldavian), and their colleague Hans Morten. Indeed, it is one of the partners' business concepts to personally welcome everyone into their store.

Torben actually started in the jewelry trade at age 16. He studied in the US, where he developed his craftsmanship and earned his certification. The shop only trades in new jewels of the highest quality, whether they are made in their own workshops, or are products of some of the most famous names in the business (such as Lapponia, Toftegaard and Baraka). The collections on display are designed to appeal to customers of all age groups. As the owners insist that clients should receive good service in their own language, Torben and Stella are fluent, between them, in English, German, Swedish, Russian, Romanian, Italian and, of course, Danish.

Pens

FYLDEPENNE DEPOTET
Nygade 6
☎ 33-11-33-22

This is one of just a few stores in Denmark that specialize in fountain pens, and you would be hard pressed to find a larger display of pens anywhere. The internationally recognized names of the brands on display flow freely onto the page: Waterman,

Parker, Sheaffer, Montblanc, Cartier, Cross, Lamy and Caran d'Ache are all represented here in every shape and size imaginable, with some commanding hefty prices. A number of these pens have become fashion statements in their own right, and now come with a whole array of expensive accessories. Also on offer are other writing accessories, such as letter openers, unusual staplers, clocks and calculators.

Souvenirs & Gifts

SVEN CARLSEN A/S
Vesterbrogade 2
☎ 33-11-73-31

There is no shortage of souvenir and gift shops in Copenhagen, but few have the vast selection that can be found in this two-level store just across from Tivoli Gardens and close to the Town Hall Square. What's more, if you ever get to meet the owner, you will find that he epitomizes the typical Danish sense of humor.

Timepieces & Weather Meters

OLE MATHIESEN
Østergade 8
☎ 33-14-12-08
www.olemathiesen.dk

The Danish sense of design and style is well known, and will be evident to every visitor to Ole Mathiesen.

The history of the Mathiesen company dates back to 1845. At that time, the company produced pocket watches and chronometers, and was a supplier to the Royal Danish Court. However, it wasn't until 1919, when Axel O. Mathiesen became head of the company, that it began to manufacture quality wristwatches.

In 1962, Axel's son Ole Mathiesen – a master watchmaker who had worked for a leading Swiss watch manufacturer – took a leading role in the company.

He set out to design a timelessly classical collection of reasonably priced watches, and he certainly achieved his objective. These ultra-flat timepieces with Swiss quartz movement, bearing the designer's initials OM1, have had the same features for over forty years. They are sold, in limited numbers, at the museum store of the Museum of Modern Art in New York and through discerning retailers in 18 other countries.

More recently, the collection has been expanded to include the first Mathiesen Sports watch (OMS1). This line retains the classic design features of the original; it is a merger of elegance and strength, and includes mechanical movement with automatic winding. Coming soon is the OMB line, meant to fill the gap between the OM1 and OMS; this will have hand-wound movement. At Ole Mathiesen, you can choose from brands like Patek Philippe, Lange & Sohne, Audemars Piguet, Breguet, Frank Muller, Girard-Perregaux, Jaeger-LeCoultre, IWC, Cartier, Bulgari, Omega and Oris, with some models selling for as much as DKK 1.5 million.

GULLACKSEN URE
Frederiksberggade 8
☎ 33-13-17-64

Another third-generation watchmaker is Niels Gullacksen. Gullacksen Ure is considered to be among the best of Copenhagen's watchmakers. In addition to a wide array of both Danish and international watches, Gullacksen Ure offers an extensive selection of watchbands, wall clocks, and alarm clocks. The shop also specializes in hygrometers (indicating humidity), barometers and thermometers.

Denmark is famous, of course, for developing products that combine style and practicality, and few are better at the art than Jacob Jensen. In his cleverly designed weather station, one vertical stand holds a barometer, a hygrometer, an alarm clock, and a thermometer. The latter receives and displays data from as many as three remote stations, which can be placed at various locations inside or outside the house. This set, high-tech and elegant, will make a unique addition to your home.

After Dark

Bars & Pubs

The Danes have made many reputations for themselves, and none of them have anything to do with abstention. In fact, quite the opposite is true. The presence of the **Carlsberg** brewery, and to a lesser extent **Tuborg**, is hard to escape in Copenhagen. It is surprising, however, that for such a small country Denmark is one of the world's leading exporters of beer.

Danish tastes in beverages extend far beyond beer. Danes are particularly fond of their own version of that famous Scandinavian spirit, **Akvavit**. This is distilled from a fermented potato or grain mash and is flavored with either caraway or cumin seed, producing a clear pale yellow drink with an alcohol content between 42% and 45% by volume.

WATER OF LIFE

Called *Akvavit* in Danish and Swedish or *Akuavit* in Norwegian, the name derives from the Latin *aqua vitae,* "water of life." *Linie Aquavit* is a famous Norwegian brand. It is so named because it is shipped to Australia and back in oak containers; supposedly, crossing the Equator (linie) gives it a mellower flavor.

It is not surprising then, that there is no shortage of places in Copenhagen where you can consume alcohol; the reality is that you simply can't miss them. The trick is, though, to find the unusual places, the small bars with interesting ambiances. The following is not a comprehensive review. These are places that appealed to this author, those that visitors to Copenhagen most probably wouldn't find by themselves.

CAFE PALUDAN
Fiolstræde 10-12
☎ 33-15-07-71

This is a neat, bright and very unusual bar in the fact that it closes at 7 pm on weeknights and 6 pm on Saturday nights, and doesn't even open on Sunday. Why recommend a bar that has such limited hours? The reason is simple: the author has never before seen a bar in a bookshop. The location, of course, accounts for the hours. If you fancy a drink while you catch up on the latest books and magazines, this is your place. On Thursdays, Café Paludan holds writers' evenings at the **Hotel Sofitel Plaza**.

Café Paludan also has a good coffee, croissant and sandwich menu.

JERNBANECAFEEN
Reventlowsgade 16
☎ 33-21-60-90

This is a typical local pub. It is just outside the Central Station, and can easily be identified by the large, lit sign saying *ØL* (meaning beer) outside. Inside, it is small and colorful, with tables crowded close together and with walls covered with paintings and model trains.

TOP OF TOWN WINE BAR
Amager Boulevard 70
☎ 33-96-58-58

Located as it is on the 25th floor of the Radisson SAS Scandinavia Hotel, this pleasant bar has one of the best views in Copenhagen. The wines are pretty good, too, with a selection of over 200. There is a daily bar menu featuring tapas and the like, and a humidor with hand-rolled Cuban and Dominican cigars. Thursday night is live samba jazz tunes night.

CHARLIE'S BAR
Pilestræde 33
☎ 33-32-22-89

Small, cozy and comfortable, and Denmark's only free house (an establishment that is not affiliated with a particular brewery and can sell what it wants), this comes as close to a traditional English pub as you are likely to find in Copenhagen (there are no TV's here). Expect to find English, Belgian and German beers, with a selection of Danish ones too. To add to the ambiance, a small keg sits on the bar awaiting your attention.

QUEEN VICTORIA
Snaregade 4
☎ 33-91-01-91

Many stars of the theater, film and TV worlds are attracted to this combination restaurant and bar. The appropriately named **Foyer Bar** is covered from wall-to-wall with signed photographs of celebrities, and it's fun to see how many you can identify.

HVIIDS VINSTUE

Kongens Nytorv 19
☎ 33-15-10-64

Located on the grand square since 1723, Hviids Vinstue, affectionately referred to by all as Hviid, continues to be a firm favorite with Copenhageners nearly three centuries later. When you step down into it, you literally step back through the ages. Wooden dividers separate sturdy wooden tables, chairs and benches, and the walls are lined with framed photographs and prints, all of which sit under formidable wooden beams. Treat yourself to a Danish open-face sandwich.

CAFE A PORTA

Kongens Nytorv 17
☎ 33-11-05-00

This is one of the city's oldest cafés; it dates from 1788, and has been popular ever since. The lovely décor has been restored to the original appearance. It's an ideal stop for a meal or a drink. A neat touch here is the cocktail menu hanging on the wall; here, besides finding new concoctions to try, feel free to add your own favorite to the list.

THE MOUSE & ELEPHANT

(*Musen & Elefanten*)
Vestergade 21
☎ 33-14-46-10

Without doubt, this quirky little bar is one of Copenhagen's more hidden secrets. It's so difficult to find, in fact, that this author – knowing what he was looking for, and where it was supposed to be – still walked past it three times!

Step down into the ground floor bar and you'll find it has a real "spit and sawdust" ambiance, with rather basic furnishings. One room on the upper floor has some tables and chairs, but the real attraction is in

If you find that you enjoy these alcoholic treats, then you can keep enjoying then until 5 am in most establishments.

the bar itself. There, mounted on a wall, is a model of an elephant's head; when the barmaid pulls the left tusk, Carlsberg Elephant beer flows smoothly into your waiting glass. This is the only place in Copenhagen where that very special beer is sold in draft form rather than in bottles. Be warned, though; Elephant Draft is much stronger than regular beer, and takes some getting used to. And, at DKK 25 for a small glass (a larger bottle in a supermarket might only be around DKK 8), it is not cheap. Of course, there are other beers to choose from, as well as the bar's own special cocktail called *Små Grå* – Little Greys. This consists of vodka with Turkish pepper and salmiak (black licorice) added; it is strong enough to pin back the ears of an elephant. After a couple of these you may think you are seeing things when the beer mats proclaim that you are in the *Elefanten & Musen*, rather than the *Musen & Elefanten*. Don't worry, however, there is a simple answer; some time ago the original bar went bust, so they started up again by changing the name around.

Casino

CASINO COPENHAGEN
Radisson SAS Scandinavia Hotel
Amager Boulevard 70
☎ 33-96-59-65, fax 33-96-59-66

This large and glitzy casino has played host to the celebrity attendees, including Pierce Brosnan, at the Danish premieres of the last two *James Bond* movies. Casino Copenhagen is open from 2 pm to 4 am; admission DKK 80. Identification such as a passport is required; the minimum age is 18. Dress code: jacket, no sportswear.

Blackjack, seven tables; Caribbean stud poker, two tables; English roulette, 10 tables; French roulette, one table; punto banco, one table; video poker, 37 machines; and 140 slot machines.

Best Places To Stay

Hotels are listed in order of the author's preference within each price range. The stars after each hotel's name reflect the **HORESTA** rating system (see page 10), which is used throughout Denmark. All hotels listed in this book accept major credit cards unless otherwise noted. Most offer a hearty Danish breakfast, which is usually included in the rate.

ACCOMMODATIONS PRICE SCALE	
Prices reflect double occupancy.	
Moderate	$100-$150
Expensive	$151-$200
Very Expensive	$201-$250
Very, Very Expensive	over $250

Very, Very Expensive

HOTEL D'ANGLETERRE ★★★★★
Kongens Nytorv 34
☎ 33-12-0095
Fax 33-12-11-18
www.remmen.dk
124 rooms

This is one of the oldest hotels in the world, with a history of service spanning over 250 years at its superb location overlooking Kongens Nytorv. As Copenhagen's finest and grandest hotel, it has hosted royalty, presidents, film stars and a host of other prominent guests. Its grand rooms are sumptuously

Hotel d'Angleterre is a member of the Leading Hotels of the World group.

furnished and boast the latest technology, including the famous GUESTNET system that allows guests to send and receive e-mail without the use of a computer. It also boats one of Copenhagen's most luxurious spa and fitness centers.

Hotel d'Angleterre was named the Best Hotel in Denmark for the six years preceding 2001, and was nominated as the seventh-best hotel in Europe by the readers of *Condé Nast Traveler*.

COPENHAGEN MARRIOTT HOTEL ★★★★★
Kalvedad Brygge, 7
☎ 61-96-49-60
Fax 61-96-49-61
404 rooms and suites

Copenhagen Marriott is the only hotel in the city with a genuine American style and ambiance.

This relatively new hotel, opened in September 2001, is on the harborfront behind Tivoli Gardens. Ask for a room on the water side for a fantastic view. The hotel has large, spacious rooms, some of which are wheelchair-accessible or non-smoking, and all of which have the latest facilities, including a data port. Other amenities include a business center, executive lounge, parking facilities, a health club, restaurants, bars and a gift shop.

FIRST HOTEL VESTERBRO ★★★★
Vesterbrogade 23-29
☎ 33-78-80-00
Fax 33-78-80-80
www.firsthotels.com
403 rooms

Single ladies should ask for one of First Hotel's 10 designated First Lady rooms.

When it opened in 1999, this was the first hotel to be built in Copenhagen for more than 15 years; at that time it was ranked the third largest in Denmark. The location is convenient – just a five-minute walk from Tivoli or Rådhuspladsen. The rooms are thoroughly modern, with air conditioning, voice mail,

ISDN outlet and Internet access via TV, and a PC safe.

For the comfort of non-smoking guests, 200 of the guest rooms and most public areas are designated non-smoking. The covered **Atrium Garden** is the social gathering place of the hotel, and also home of the IT@First business center.

HILTON COPENHAGEN AIRPORT ★★★★★
Ellehammersvej 20
☎ 32-50-15-01
Fax 32-52-85-28
382 rooms, 12 floors

This hotel was opened in 2001. It was the first Hilton in Scandinavia. The hotel is directly connected to the airport by a covered walkway. The design consists of four towers surrounding a 45-m (147-ft) atrium, epitomizing all the best aspects of Danish architecture, decorative art, design and colors. The rooms are the largest of any hotel in Copenhagen, ranging from 32 sq m (344 sq ft) for the Standard up to 48 sq m (516 sq ft) for Junior Suites and a massive 160 sq m (1,722 sq ft) for the Presidential Suite. All of them have the latest features. Amenities include Bang & Olufsen TV, separate bath and shower, and individually controlled air conditioning. Some rooms are designated as allergy-friendly. The hotel also has several restaurants with clearly different identities, and a fitness room incorporating a pool, steam room and sauna.

RADISSON SAS ROYAL ★★★★★
Hammerichsgade 1
☎ 33-42-60-00
Fax 33-42-61-00
www.radissonsas.com
265 rooms

This Arne Jacobsen-designed high-rise hotel dating from 1960 is decorated in understated luxury with a Danish Modern design. From many of the guest rooms, and from the 20th-floor Summit Restaurant, there are spectacular panoramic views of Tivoli Gardens and the city. Guests also have the use of the Netpoint Royal IT Center, an exercise room, sauna and solarium.

RADISSON SCANDINAVIA HOTEL ★★★★
Amager Boulevard 70
☎ 33-96-50-00
Fax 33-96-55-00
www.radissonsas.com
542 rooms, 25 floors

Request a room on one of the Radisson Scandinavia's upper floors to get an amazing view of Copenhagen and the surrounding areas.

Just across the harbor and about a 10-minute walk from downtown, this massive 25-story hotel dominates the skyline. The rooms have every modern feature and are furnished in Standard, Scandinavian or Oriental décor. Discriminating guests will find extra refinements in Business Class rooms. The Form & Fitness Center includes an indoor pool, squash courts and a sauna. Entertainment is available in the Casino Copenhagen, found on the ground floor. The array of restaurants includes Italian, an American Steak House and a Japanese, as well as the acclaimed **Blue Elephant** for Thai cuisine, featuring seafood flown in fresh from the Gulf of Siam.

IMPERIAL HOTEL ★★★★

Vester Farimagsgade 9
☎ 33-12-80-00
Fax 33-93-80 31
www.imperialhotel.dk
163 rooms

This hotel is next door to the Vesterport train station, a few minutes walk from Rådhuspladsen. Its rooms, rated Standard, Top Class or Deluxe, are modern, well appointed and feature Danish design and art; the décor is enhanced with flowers and green plants. Some floors are designated as smoke-free. On-site dining includes the **Restaurant Imperial Garden** and the **Brasserie Imperial**.

Copenhagen

TELEPHONE TIP

Telephone numbers as listed are local. To make reservations when calling from the US, you must first dial 011-45 and then the number we've listed.

Very Expensive

SOFITEL PLAZA HOTEL ★★★★

Bernstorffsgade 4
☎ 33-14-92-62
Fax 33-93-93-62
www.accorhotel.dk
93 rooms

This hotel, commissioned in 1913 by King Frederick VIII, offers a location close to Central Station. It has beautifully appointed rooms and traditional décor throughout. Its attractive **Library Bar** has been voted one of the five best bars in the world by *Forbes* magazine. Enjoy a Scandinavian breakfast buffet in the **Flora Danica Brasserie**.

Non-smoking rooms are available at the Sofitel Plaza.

HOTEL KONG FREDERIK ★★★★
Vester Voldgade 25
☎ 33-12-59-02
Fax 33-93-59-01
www.remmen.dk
110 rooms

The current Hotel Kong Frederik was created in 1976 when it merged with the adjacent Hotel Hafnia. These two small hotels had been in operation as competitors since the 19th century, in buildings dating from the 14th century. The hotel was most recently renovated in 1993 when it was purchased by the Remmens, a family of hoteliers. The hotels still retain their classic English ambiance, but all rooms now offer the latest technology, including the GUESTNET system, which allows access to and sending of e-mails without the use of a computer.

GRAND HOTEL ★★★★
Vesterbrogade 9A
☎ 33-31-36-00
Fax 33-31-33-50
www.grandhotelcopenhagen.dk
161 rooms

Corner rooms at the Grand offer slightly more space than others.

The Grand Hotel, dating from 1890, has an enticing façade and boasts a prestigious corner location on an important street. Its rooms and suites were updated and tastefully renovated in 1998, in a manner that has preserved much of their original character. The on-site **Restaurant Oliver** presents Danish-French cuisine, and the **Grand Bar** has a French-style outdoor café open from May to September.

MAYFAIR HOTEL ★★★
Helgolandsgade 3
☎ 33-31-48-01
Fax 33-23-96-86
106 rooms

The Mayfair is a turn-of-the-century hotel that has been refurbished and updated. Each room is comfortably furnished in classical English style, enhanced with Far Eastern furniture. Pleasant extras include complimentary tea and coffee in the lounge and use of the hotel's Internet connection for e-mail or other purposes; rooms are outfitted with a PC outlet. Thirty rooms are designated non-smoking. The hotel is just two blocks from the Central Station.

HOTEL CITY ★★★
Peder Skramsgade 24
☎ 33-13-06-66
Fax 33-13-06-67
www.hotelcity.dk
81 rooms

Hotel City is discreetly elegant, with a striking modern décor; rooms are tastefully furnished to international standards. It is housed in an elegant townhouse, in an interesting area of Copenhagen near Nyhavn and the hydrofoil boats to Malmö, Sweden.

Hotel City, a member of the organic food organization, Green Key, offers some organic products in the breakfast buffet.

COPENHAGEN STRAND ★★★
Havnegade 37
☎ 33-48-99-00
Fax 33-48-99-01
www.copenhagenstrand.dk
174 rooms

This ultra-modern hotel, opened in July 2000, is housed in a converted warehouse dating from 1869. It's on a side street just off Nyhavn, close to Kongens Nytorv.

HOTEL ALEXANDRA ★★★
H.C. Andersens Boulevard 8
☎ 33-74-44-44
Fax 33-74-44-88
www.hotel-alexandra.dk
61 rooms

The Alexandra is a lovely old hotel in a building originating from 1880; it is almost next door to Rådhuspladsen. Rooms are light, airy and pleasantly decorated, and the hotel has excellent facilities and amenities, including designated non-smoking and allergy-friendly rooms.

Expensive

SOPHIE AMALIE HOTEL ★★★★
Sankt Annæ Plads 21
☎ 33-13-34-00
Fax 33-11-77-07
www.remmen.dk
134 rooms

The Sophie Amalie was named in honor of the 17th-century queen who gained popularity when she refused to leave Copenhagen during the Swedish siege.

Between the Amalienborg Palace and Nyhavn, the Sophie Amalie was built in 1948 as the Codan Hotel. The hotel was renamed by the Remmen family, who purchased it in 1984 and reopened it in 1986 after a two-year renovation. The Sophie Amalie has comfortable and well-equipped rooms; amenities include the GUESTNET system.

IBSENS HOTEL ★★★
Vendersgade 23,
☎ 33-13-19-13
Fax 33-13-19-16
101 rooms

Ibsens is a small but very comfortable hotel that has recently been renovated. It is in a pleasant neighborhood about a 15-minute walk from the city center, between Nørreport Station and Peblinge Lake.

COPENHAGEN ADMIRAL HOTEL ★★★★
Tolbodgade 24-28
☎ 33-74-14-14
Fax 33-74-14-16
www.admiral-hotel.dk
366 rooms

The Copenhagen Admiral is housed in a building that dates from 1787, when it functioned as a granary, and it still retains the ambiance of that era. Each room is unique in character; Junior Suites, for example, feature spiral staircases ascending from sitting room to bedroom. As befits its name, the hotel is beside the harbor in a building that survived both the Battle of Copenhagen in 1801 and the British bombardment six years later. Amenities include the **Pinafore** restaurant, **Nautilus** nightclub, and a sauna and solarium. The Copenhagen Admiral is notable for the 200-year-old Pomeranian pine beams that span the guest rooms and public areas.

HOTEL ASTORIA ★★★
Banegårdspladsen 4
☎ 33-14-14-19
Fax 33-14-08-02
www.astoriahotelcopenhagen.dk
94 rooms

The Astoria is a cubist-style, low-rise, rectangular structure dating from 1936. Now, almost 70 years later, it looks somewhat dated. However, the 94 rooms have been updated to appeal to modern tastes. Rooms are organized into different categories; some, with up to five beds, are suitable for families.

The strange statue – a wheel with wings – on the roof of the Astoria is the symbol of the Danish railways.

Moderate

IBIS COPENHAGEN STAR ★★★

Colbjørnsensgade 13
☎ 33-22-11-00
Fax 33-21-21-86
www.accorhotel.dk
134 rooms

The Ibis Copenhagen Star is one of the hotels in a cluster of streets near the railroad station, a few blocks from Tivoli. This one has well-appointed and clean rooms, including some that are designated as non-smoking, and even an inviting Jacuzzi.

Best Places To Eat

With over 2,000 restaurants, many of them serving ethnic cuisine, Copenhagen is something of a gourmet's paradise. This applies particularly to the establishments that have been awarded **Michelin** stars. Whether you fancy a quick coffee and *wienerbrød* or a five-course feast, you'll have plenty of places to choose from. There are over 30 eating establishments inside the **Tivoli Gardens** alone, and nearby is the **Scala Centre**, with numerous bars and restaurants of all types. For lunch, cafés offer the best option for economy-minded diners, with a selection of hot dishes and filling *smørrebrød* at reasonable prices. Dinner can be as light or as heavy as you like, and many places offer the traditional Scandinavian open table, where you eat as much as you wish for a set charge.

Note that the high import duty on wines can add considerably to the final bill.

The first category of restaurants listed below are those with Michelin ratings. The next group includes some classy, and very expensive, restaurants, some of which are quite trendy. Following these is a listing of restaurants in the middle- to upper-level price range and, finally, a handful of inexpensive selections.

In addition to the Michelin-rated restaurants (these, naturally, are all covered here) the remaining selections are a cross-section of what is available and are, in fact, the author's favorites.

Because of the high cost of wine, it is difficult to set a price range for these restaurants. Suffice it to say, however, that for Michelin-rated establishments you can expect to pay between DKK 750 and DKK 1,000 for a dinner for one with wine. Prices at the better restaurants, even those without a Michelin star, can come very close to DKK 1,000 as well, although if you choose less expensive wines it is more likely to cost between DKK 500 and DKK 750. The choice of wine will affect the cost of a meal at the moderately-priced restaurants as well, where main dishes might cost between DKK 125 and DKK 200. There aren't that many inexpensive places to eat in Copenhagen, but at those recommended here the price for a meal will generally be between DKK 50 and DKK 150, without drinks. For an up-to-date listing of eating establishments, consult the free monthly *Copenhagen This Week* (see page 130).

Copenhagen

Michelin-Rated Restaurants

KOMMANDANTEN ★★
Ny Adelgade, 7
☎ 33-12-09-90 or www.kommandanten.dk

Kommandanten is in a 1698 townhouse that once served as the residence of the commander of Copenhagen. The restaurant has numerous small rooms decorated with hand-made iron furniture and accented with floral arrangements by the imaginative and legendary Tage Andersen, an interior designer whose futuristic studio is just across the street.

Kommandanten is the only restaurant in Denmark with a Michelin rating of two stars.

The house specialty is the Kommandantens Menu, at DKK 690 per person, which consists of six small courses. The menu changes every two weeks, as it is created with seasonal produce chosen directly from the market. The à la carte menu is not extensive, but offers such tempting and beautifully presented dishes as smoked Irish salmon served with oysters; oyster cream and herb salad; and grilled sole served with spinach and lobster ravioli. Needless to say, the wine list, one of the most extensive in Copenhagen, is simply amazing, with an entire page of champagnes and a fine international influence.

RESTAURATIONEN ★
Møntergade, 19
☎ 33-14-94-95

At Restaurationen, the selections will be described in delectable detail at your table by Bo – or by his able young deputy – using an easel and board.

The word restaurant – and the name of this restaurant – originate from the term meaning "to restore" and, since opening their establishement in 1991, that is exactly what charismatic owners, Bo & Lisbeth Jacobsen, have endeavored to do: to restore each guest's spirits so they leave feeling happy and contented. To this end, Restaurationen offers a single five-course fixed menu. Only the freshest seasonal produce is used. The menu alternates between summer and winter themes, with wines carefully selected to enhance the food. The menu changes weekly; the cost is around DKK 1,000 per person.

The restaurant's wine list has over 750 selections; the cheese trolley has over 30 different Danish and international varieties. One cheese selection or one glass of wine is an additional DKK 25-30 (vintage wine is available by the glass for DKK 125).

KONG HANS KÆLDER ★
Vingaardsstræde, 6
☎ 33-11-68-68 or www.konghans.dk

This restaurant, housed in the oldest building in Copenhagen (it dates from sometime in the 13th century, but not even the current owners know the exact date), features dining areas graced by Gothic arches, giving it a decidedly medieval ambiance. It is appropriate, then, that it is named for King Hans, an early 16th-century monarch.

Copenhagen

The cuisine is reflective of classic French gastronomy with international inspirations. The Traditional menu consists of four courses and costs DKK 545 per person. The Innovation menu, at DKK 790, boasts six small courses using the best available products from around the world; the accompanying Innovation Wine menu, priced at DKK 490, features six different and especially chosen wines to accompany the courses. Prices for the Innovation dinners are per person, with a minimum of two people. Rounding out the offerings is the Signature menu; it features an array of individually priced specialties.

The restaurant Kong Hans Kælder is unique in that there is a private salmon smokehouse on the property.

In days gone by, grapes were actually cultivated on this street, hence its name: Vineyard Street. Today, the wines at Kong Hans Kælder, though chosen directly from the vineyards, are imported.

PIERRE ANDRE ★
Ny Østergade 21
☎ 33-16-17-19

Pierre André is named after Sussie and Phillip Houdet's two sons; it gained recognition very quickly after opening in 1996, and was awarded its Michelin star after just a year.

The restaurant has a 35-seat dining room with a décor featuring terracotta colors. The cuisine is a combination of modern French and classic Italian;

the menu changes periodically to adjust for the seasons. The Menu Découverte is a special dining experience consisting of nine small courses designed by the chef; it must be ordered before 8:30 pm, by everyone at the table. This dinner costs DKK 675 per person. Pierre André also offers a Dégustation menu at DKK 495, or you may order à la carte.

Not wanting to leave their daughter out of things, the owners have named the dessert menu Céline-Margaux after her; all the breads, cakes and sweets at Pierre André are homemade. As you would expect, there is also an exceptional wine list.

ERA ORA ★
Torvegade 62
☎ 32-54-06-93

Era Ora's wine cellar has a collection of 90,000 bottles; you can visit the cellar to choose your vintage if none of the 600 or so on the wine list suits your taste.

Era Ora is in a historic house facing the Christianshavn canal; it has been furnished innovatively with modern art on the walls and crystal, porcelain and silver from Italy on the tables. The menu, adapted daily according to the supply of fresh and authentic produce, is presented in the traditional Italian format, with antipasti, pasta, a main course of meat or fish, cheese and dessert. Menu ingredients are often imported from Italy. Three courses cost DKK 540 per person; four courses cost DKK 595; five courses cost DKK 650; and six courses cost DKK 750. In 1996, when Era Ora received its rating from Michelin, it was the only Italian restaurant outside Italy to earn a star.

RESTAURANT GODT ★
Gothersgade 38
☎ 33-15-21-22

Godt means Good, and that is an understatement for this small (20-seat) family-run restaurant. The ambiance here is very friendly and personal, and despite the ever-increasing popularity of the restaurant, the owners have resisted the impulse to expand the number of seats. The cuisine is European and seasonal, even including small game, such as hare, with one daily four-course menu for DKK 480. The wine list is international, and there is a daily dégustation wine menu for DKK 350 per person.

Expensive

1.TH
Heluf Trollesgade 9, 1.th
☎ 33-93-57-70

The unusual name of this restaurant is the Danish abbreviation for "first floor," and that is not the only unusual thing about it. First is its location; it is tucked away, one flight above street level, in a rather undistinguished building behind the Royal Theater. You will find it by entering from a very plain courtyard in this quiet street. Perhaps the most unusual aspect of dining here is the dinner party theme developed by owner Mette Martinussen. Guests – no more than 24 – have to book their reservation well in advance, and are invited to appear at 7 pm. Don't be late, as these hosts lock the door soon after that time.

Drinks are served in the lounge, then guests are shown to their tables ready for a delightful meal. Menus are composed at the discretion of the chef, and can have as many as 10 to 13 eclectic dishes; these are washed down with five to seven wines, at a combined cost for the evening of DKK 990 per person. Some of the dishes are likely to be quite unusual, too; a typical menu might include a presentation of fish, shellfish, venison sausages, cheese and fruit, desserts, and a selection of delicious homemade breads. Mette doesn't hurry her guests, either; expect this culinary treat to last until around 11:30 pm.

BAGATALLEN
Vesterbrogade, 33
☎ 33-75-07-51 or www.bagatallen.dk

Bagatallen, in Tivoli Gardens, is in an unusual building with an intriguing history. It was originally built as a **dance hall** in 1893. In 1912 an inner ring was added to function as a **hippodrome**, allowing audience members to test their prowess on horseback – or simply to enjoy the spectacle. Four years later a **tea room** – with a panoramic view overlooking Tivoli – was added to the hippodrome. It continued to serve that purpose, undergoing one or two renovations, until 1997, when the entire property was converted into a **gourmet restaurant**. Today, under the management of new owners who have effected yet another extensive renovation, diners can sample exquisite French-Californian cuisine while enjoying lovely views across Tivoli Lake. The dinner menu has on offer an enticing list of dishes, including Iranian sevruga caviar as a starter and a wide selection of fresh fish that varies daily.

In accordance with tradition, pastry and coffee are offered in Bagatallen's old-fashioned Tea Room each afternoon.

BLUE ELEPHANT
Amager Boulevard 70
☎ 33-96-59-70

The prestigious Blue Elephant chain of restaurants has branches in Bangkok, Brussels, Beirut, London, Malta, Paris, Lyon, New Delhi and Dubai; this branch, in the Radisson SAS Scandinavia Hotel, is probably the most unusual – and stunningly attractive – restaurant in Copenhagen; it is designed as a small Thai village with traditional houses, covered with bamboo roofing and trellised siding, set around a market place and a waterfall, all indoors.

The cuisine will not disappoint; the menu is authentic, with some ingredients flown in daily from Thailand. Whether you select individual dishes, or choose to have one of the expansive set meals, you will be presented with courses that are as attractive to your palate as the décor is to your eyes.

FORMEL B
Vesterbrogade 182
☎ 33-25-10-66

Don't let the fact that this restaurant is located in Frederiksberg – a couple of miles away from the city center – put you off going; that would be a big mistake. The décor is minimalist in the extreme, but tastefully so. The dining room consists of an L-shaped space; a mix of table sizes accommodates 25 people. Wine is stored in racks built into the wall. At the bar you can have your meal while talking to the chefs preparing your food just a few feet away. In the summer there are tables outside, raising the capacity to 60.

Then, of course, there's the cuisine, called Funky French by the owners. Dishes are beautifully prepared and presented. There is just one menu, which changes every Monday. It consists of courses such as roasted mullet with chanterelles and almonds, or terrine of crabs and mussels with beetroot. You may choose four courses at DKK 425; five at DKK 450; or the full six courses for DKK 495. The wine list has over 200 selections, including over 20 champagnes, and 25 are sold by the glass.

To keep you occupied while waiting for your meal at Formel B, there is a large backgammon board built into the ground.

KROGS FISKERRESTAURANT
Gammel Strand, 38
☎ 33-15-89-15 or www.krogs.com

Krogs is regarded as the finest fish restaurant in Copenhagen; it is justly renowned for its excellent seafood menu. The restaurant, in a prestigious location overlooking the canal and Christiansborg, is housed in an 18th-century building that has been updated with early 20th-century décor.

Wine connoisseurs will be interested to learn that Krogs was the first restaurant in Copenhagen to employ a sommelier.

Start with cold or hot caviar appetizers before selecting fish or shellfish dishes from the à la carte menu. If you opt for the Krogs menu, you'll be presented with a selection of five courses at DKK 645, with one glass of wine per course for an extra DKK 495. Another option, the Grand Surprise menu, consists of small courses made from seasonal produce; it must be ordered before 9 pm by everyone at the table, and the cost is DKK 875 per person.

RESTAURANT PS
Store Kongensgade 52
☎ 33-11-50-17 or www.restaurantps.dk

Relax before, during or after your meal in the lounge at Restaurant PS. You are also invited to take a beer into the kitchen and have a chat with Simon.

This is one of Copenhagen's innovative new restaurants. The young English chef, Simon Sheard, has developed a style he calls Pan Pacific; it incorporates continental, Australian and Asian influences. There is only one menu, with dishes that might include such delicacies as monkfish on ravioli of pequilo-peppers with sauce velouté of smoked paprika. You can select three courses for DKK 365; four courses for DKK 405; five courses for DKK 465; or six courses for DKK 525. Wine by the glass is extra, with most selections between DKK 50 and DKK 85. If you have any special requests, such as a vegetarian meal, call Simon a few days in advance and he'll take care of it.

SØREN K
Søren Kierkegaards Plads 1
☎ 33-47-49-49

Søren K has maximized the art of being minimalist.

As you might expect from a restaurant that is located in the Black Diamond (see page 27), this is a modern place. The dining room is long and narrow, with booths against the wall; tables are closer to the tall windows, allowing magnificent views over the harbor. In the summer you may opt to eat on the terrace.

Søren K has carved out for itself, in a comparatively short time, a reputation for fine international cuisine. The dishes here are creative and well presented, offering an amazing combination of tastes. Main courses are DKK 185, and a set meal with four courses costs DKK 330 (wine is extra, of course).

Moderate

Copenhagen

A HEREFORD BEEFSTOUW
Tivoli, Vesterbrogade, 3
☎ 33-12-74-41

This is part of a chain of steakhouses and, as such, normally would not be included in a guide such as this. However, as its locations indicate – throughout Denmark, in Hamburg, in Göteborg and at Hong Kong International Airport – this is no ordinary chain. Not only does the management design, and often construct, all that is needed in the way of furniture and fittings, but a percentage of the profits is invested in the artwork that adorns the restaurants. They serve up, as the name implies, thick juicy steaks, which are often brought in from Australia. Diners will be tempted too by Baltic salmon and lobster (*hummer*) plates and a fine salad bar that can be chosen as a side or a main dish. The brewery next door, Bryggeriet Apollo, is also a part of the chain (as are the breweries in Århus and Herning) and the organic and seasonal brews are well worth tasting.

The beer of the month at A Hereford Beefstouw sells for DKK 25 a ¼ liter.

CAFE LUMSKEBUGTEN
Esplanaden, 21
☎ 33-15-60-29

This is a small, but rather exclusive, restaurant, located just past Amalienborg and across from Churchill Park. It has a rather distinguished clientele; in fact, until his death in 1947, King Christian X was a regular customer.

The name Lumskebugten means "treacherous bay."

By tradition, the restaurant is charged with the responsibility for the **Royal Barge** that is moored nearby. This accounts for the photos and models of watercraft which adorn the bar and restaurant.

In fine weather, the café's waterfront location makes it a charming place for lunch or dinner at one of the outdoor tables. Traditional seafood dishes dominate the menu, along with Russian caviar and a smattering of beef and veal plates. One unusual combination is tatar of beef with lemon cream and Russian caviar.

CAVIAR HOUSE CVH SEAFOOD BAR
Holegaard
Amagertorv 8
☎ 38-14-96-37

Magasin
Kongens Nytorv 13
☎ 33-18-24-10

Caviar House is a well-known restaurant chain. Most of its branches are at major airports, but these two seafood bars are a new, and novel, addition to the Copenhagen restaurant scene. Both are in important stores, with the former – more formal – in the Royal Copenhagen complex and the latter in the basement of the newly renovated and designed Magasin Department store. The array of seafood, and of course caviar, is tempting indeed. The wine list at both is more than adequate, and the branch in Magasin can call on the much larger resources of that company's famous Food and Wine Department. These are great places for lunch, but don't plan on a late dinner, as their hours are the same as those of the stores.

GRÅBRØDRE TORV 21
Gråbrødretorv, 21
☎ 33-11-47-07

This restaurant is in a charming house on Grey Friars' Square, from which it gets its name. Whether you choose to be seated in one of the old-fashioned rooms or outdoors on the terrace, dining here is delightful. Classical Danish specialties, prepared and presented nicely, comprise both the lunch and dinner menus. DKK 350 (without wine).

LE SOMMELIER
Bredgade 63-65
☎ 33-11-45-15 or www.lesommelier.dk

Le Sommelier occupies a very large space, which includes a bar and a dining area. Expect mussels, oysters and pâté de foie gras for starters, and a choice of eclectic entrées, such as pigeon or suckling pig, as well as veal, lamb and fish, for your main course. Forty wines are available by the glass; reputedly, the restaurant has the largest cellar in Denmark.

Le Sommelier won the Wine Spectator *Best Award of Excellence in 1999.*

Inexpensive

ASTOR DEEP PAN PIZZA RESTAURANT
Vesterbrogade 7
☎ 33-14-90-14

Astor Pizza is on the ground floor of the Hotel Astor. This is one of the cheapest places in town, serving pizza and salad for a little over DKK 50; prices are even lower before 5 pm.

BISTRO
Banegårdspladsen 7
☎ 33-69-21-12

Set in the imposing marble-columned, vaulted railroad station, Bistro is famous for its traditional

Station yourself at Bistro for a good, inexpensive, meal.

Danish cuisine; the all-you-can-eat Bistro Buffet is available for DKK 129 per person.

GOVINDAS VEGETAR RESTAURANT
Nørre Farimagsgade 82
☎ 33-33-74-44

Govindas is a small, unpretentious vegetarian restaurant; it is close to the Botanisk Have. Dinner is about DKK 60 (without drinks).

INDIA PALACE
H.C. Andersens Boulevard 13
☎ 33-91-04-08

You'll find this authentic Indian restaurant, with extremely tempting cuisine served in pleasant surroundings, just a short step from Rådhuspladsen. The restaurant's delicious all-you-can-eat lunch is DKK 59; dinner is DKK 115. The buffets are extremely popular and are an excellent value.

KØBENHAVNER CAFEEN
Badstuestræde, 10
☎ 33-32-80-81

Just off Strøget, this charming restaurant is typically Danish; it is particularly recommended for its daily Copenhagen Plate, with six items for a little over DKK 100. Regional dishes include roast pork and meat balls, each served with red cabbage and boiled potatoes.

MONGOLIAN BARBECUE
Stormgade 35
☎ 33-14-63-20

The buffet at Mongolian Barbecue, serving steak, pork, chicken and lamb with vegetables and spices, is an excellent value, with as much as you can eat for around DKK 100.

NYHAVNS FÆRGEKRO
Nyhavn, 5
☎ 33-15-15-88

The **Ferry Inn**, as the name is translated, is one of many restaurants along the famous Nyhavn; this one is unpretentious and full of character, and has established a reputation for serving particularly good traditional food. It is especially famous for its herring buffet. Also popular are the *smørrebrød* (sandwiches) and salads, though raw herring, a specialty here, is very much an acquired taste.

Copenhagen Information

Embassies & Consulates

Embassies are generally open Monday to Friday from 8 am to 4 pm; there is usually a 24-hour telephone service.

USA

Embassy and **Consulate**, Dag Hammarskjölds Allé 24, DK-2100 Copenhagen Ø, ☎ 35-55-31-44.

Canada

Embassy, Kristen Bernikowsgade 1, DK-1105 Copenhagen K; ☎ 33-48-32-00, fax 33-48-32-20.

UK

Embassy and **Consulate**, Kastelsvej 40, DK-2100 Copenhagen Ø; ☎ 35-44-52-00, fax 35-44-52-53.

Emergencies

Ambulance, police & fire . . . . ☎ 112

Doctors are on call on weekdays, 8 am to 4 pm; ☎ 33-93-63-00. Outside these hours, call ☎ 38-88-60-41.

For **dental emergencies**, an organization called Tandlægevagten, at Oslo Plads, 14, is open year-round. Hours are 8 am to 9:30 pm on weekdays, 10 am to noon on Saturdays, Sundays and public holidays. ☎ 35-38-02-51.

Pharmacies are listed in the trade phone book under *Apoteker*. Hours are from 9 am to 5:30 pm, and until 1 pm on Saturday. All-night service is available at **Steno Apotek**, 69, Vesterbrogade, ☎ 33-14-82-66; and at **Sønderbro Apotek**, 158, Amangerbrog, ☎ 32-58-01-40.

English Language Publications

Copenhagen This Week is an official weekly English language booklet; it is readily available at hotels and other places of business, and is essential reading for visitors to Copenhagen; www.ctw.dk.

The Copenhagen Post is a free weekly English language newspaper; it is available at airlines, hotels, restaurants and certain stores every Friday.

Tourist In Copenhagen is a colorful, highly informative and free booklet. It is published annually and offers detailed information, maps and plans of Copenhagen and the surrounding areas.

Lost Property

The general lost-property office (*hittegodskontor*) is at the **police station** at 113, Slotsherrensvej, Vanløse, ☎ 38-74-52-61. It is open Monday to Thursday, 9 am to 5:30 pm; and Friday, 9 am to 2 pm.

For property lost in buses or trains, contact **HT** at Lyshøjgårdsvej 80, Valby, ☎ 36-13-14-15; the office is open daily, 7 am to 9:30 pm.

Police

State and **city police** all form part of the national force; all are in black uniforms. Some walk their beat through central Copenhagen, but most policemen patrol in deep-blue-and-white or all-white cars with the word *POLITI* in large letters (they also tend to roam around in unmarked cars). You're entitled to stop police cars at any time and request help. Police are courteous, and all speak English – they take a mandatory 80 English lessons during training.

All local stations are listed in the phone book under *Politi*; don't hesitate to go to them if in need of advice.

Post Offices

The **main branch**, at 35-39, Tietgensgade (just behind Tivoli), is open Monday to Friday, 11 am to 6 pm; and Saturday, 10 am to 1 pm. The post office at the Central Station has longer hours: Monday to Friday, 8 am to 10 pm; Saturday, 9 am to 4 pm; and Sunday, 10 am to 5 pm.

There are also numerous sub-offices around town; these are identifiable by a red sign with a crown, bugle, and crossed arrows in yellow, and a sign saying *Kongelig Post og Telegraf*. Danish postboxes, bright red, stand out clearly along the street.

Places of Worship

The official Danish church is Protestant (**Danish Lutheran Evangelical**), and 92% of Danes are members.

Sunday services in English are held in the following places of worship:

Church of England

ST. ALBANS ANGLICAN EPISCOPAL CHURCH
Churchillparken
Langelinie
☎ 39-62-77-36

Sunday morning services are Holy Communion at 9 am, and Family Eucharist at 10:30 am. Wednesday morning Holy Communion is held at 10:30 am.

Roman Catholic

SACRAMENT'S CHURCH
(*Sakramentskirken*)
Nørrebrogade, 27
☎ 35-35-68-25

Services in English are held Sunday at 6 pm, and Wednesday at 5 pm.

Jewish

GREAT SYNAGOGUE
Krystalgade, 12
☎ 33-12-88-68

Services are held Friday at sundown, and Saturday at 9 pm.

Mormon

LATTER DAY SAINTS
Nitivej, 63
☎ 38-34-10-21

Services are held on Sunday, at 10 am.

Tourist Office

COPENHAGEN TOURIST INFORMATION OFFICE
Bernstorffsgade, 1
☎ 70-22-24-42
Fax 70-22-24-52
www.woco.dk, touristinfo@woco.dk

In addition to offering a comprehensive array of tourist information, such as brochures, posters and postcards, the helpful staff also offers personal assistance with booking tours and arranging hotel or private accommodations. The tourist office is also one of the many places where you can, and should, purchase the very useful **Copenhagen Card**.

The office is across from Central Station and just outside Tivoli. Between May and August, opening hours are Monday to Saturday, 9 am to 8 pm; and Sunday, 10 am to 8 pm. Other times of the year it is open Monday to Saturday from 9 am to 4:30 pm.

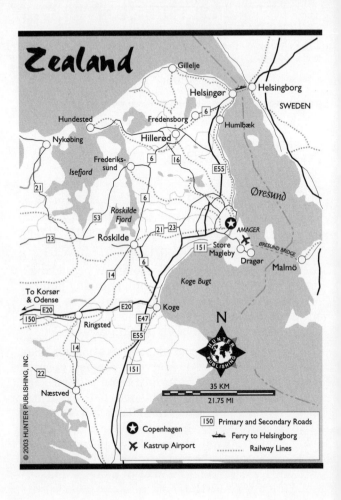

Helsingør

Helsingør, also known as **Elsinore**, owes its prominence to just one thing – its strategic location on the northern tip of Zealand (*Sjælland*), at the narrowest part of the Øresund separating Denmark from Sweden. It stands, effectively, at the entranceway to the Baltic Sea.

A Brief History

Helsingør received its charter from the hands of Erik of Pomerania in 1426. The city's considerable wealth was derived from the Sound Dues imposed on ships passing through the Øresund. These duties, instituted by Erik, were the source of enormous contributions to the Crown treasury, and Kronborg Castle was built by Erik to enforce their collection. The success of this tax gave rise to a class of well-to-do customs officers and agents, known as customs clearers; these agents, who often came from other seafaring countries, built many of the grand homes that can still be seen in the city today. It was the job of the agents to ferret out clients for themselves from among the vessels at anchor. They would facilitate the payment of the complicated taxes in exchange for fresh provisions from Helsingør's warehouses. In those days, everyday life in Helsingør focused almost exclusively on these maritime connections. There were numerous rough and ready bars for the ordinary sailors, and a number of more elegant establishments where the captains of the vessels were lavishly entertained by the agents.

Following the phasing out of the Sound Dues in the late 19th century, Helsingør entered a period of decline. It wasn't until the late 18th century that a small harbor was built. Expansion of the harbor several times throughout that century led, in the early 1880s, to the opening of the Helsingør Shipyard, which provided the main opportunities for employment until its demise in the late 20th century. Taking on the challenges presented by a rather rundown Helsingør, the local authorities, in 1971, instituted a plan to renew the town while preserving its historical charm. This they have most certainly achieved.

The City Today

Although the main attraction for visitors is certainly **Kronborg Castle**, few will leave disappointed with the town itself. Admittedly there are no other really important monuments, but Helsingør is a compact place and a short walk around it brings home the delightful ambiance that comes from its maritime history. It also offers convenient connections with Sweden. A short visit to Helsingborg, Sweden – just 20 minutes across the Øresund by ferry (see pages 139 to 140) – is always of interest and offers an opportunity to experience the contrasts between the cities and, indeed, the countries. As a final suggestion, if at all possible, plan to make your visit to Helsingør on a Saturday in summer. It is on those days that you will become part of a social phenomenon as hordes of Swedes peacefully invade Helsingør to stock up on duty-free liquor.

Getting Here

By Train

There are three S-Train departures each hour to Helsingør from Central Station in Copenhagen, with a travel time of just less than one hour, through attractive countryside. The Copenhagen Card is valid for this trip. ☎ 49-21-12-55.

By Boat

The **Sundbusserne** line (☎ 48-21-35-45) operates the smallest of the ferries plying their way between Helsingør and Helsingborg. They are this author's favorites.

Ferries are also operated by **Scandlines**, ☎ 33-15-15-15, and **HH Ferries**, ☎ 49-26-01-55, www.hhferries.dk.

Round-The-Sound

Contact the **rail** or **ferry** lines listed above, or the **tourist information office** (page 151), for information about travel between Copenhagen, Helsingør, Helsingborg and Malmö.

Sunup To Sundown

A Stroll Around Helsingør

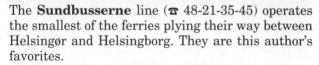

Kronborg Castle beckons. Although it's a fair walk from the station, the image of the castle will be alluring enough to encourage you. And you'll encounter a generous handful of distractions along the way.

The Harbor Area

Start at the **Helsingør Train Station**, the terminal for trains from Copenhagen and Hillerød. Upon leaving the station, the maritime influence in Helsingør immediately becomes apparent. To the right is the large Scandlines harbor, and the smaller terminal for the Sundbusserne and HH Ferries is straight ahead. Beyond those rises the dominating outline of

Helsingør's most important monument, historic
Kronborg Castle.

From the station, cross to the left to **Havnepladsen**
where, on Saturday, there is a small market; stop in
at the adjacent tourist office to gather information
about Helsingør. Then have a brief tour of the town
before heading to the castle.

THEY ARE HERE FOR THE BEER!

Even at this early stage of your acquaintance
with Helsingør, a strange phenomenon will be
apparent – the large number of stores selling
every kind of alcohol. These aren't here primarily for Danish use. Sweden, just a few minutes across the Øresund, has much stricter
regulations and much higher prices for alcohol
than Denmark (as do Norway and Finland).
Consequently, especially on Saturdays during
the summer, Helsingør is overrun with Swedes
picking up their duty-free alcohol allowances.

Until just a few years ago, Swedish visitors
were only allowed one six-pack of beer and a
little wine for every crossing, and it was a common joke that they would go back and forth on
the ferries to stock up. These days the rules
have been relaxed somewhat. This, though,
creates the logistical problem of how to carry
ones purchases, and the solution creates a
strange sight indeed. It is common to see vast
numbers of Swedes walking around Helsingør
pushing small, two-wheeled trolleys loaded
with cases of empty beer bottles. These will be
exchanged for full ones – there is a deposit on
each bottle – before embarkation for the trip
home. The store directly outside the *Sundbusserne* and HH terminal probably has the most
thriving business, as thirsty Swedes have less
distance to haul away their bargains.

Amalienborg Palace Guard.
(Norman P.T. Renouf)

Above: *Elephant Gate, Holmens Kirke.*
Below: *Tivoli Boys Guard.*
(Both photos: Norman P.T. Renouf)

Above: *Caritas Fountain.*
Below: *Traditional Guild Coat of Arms.*
(Both photos: Norman P.T. Renouf)

Above: *Statue of Hans Christian Andersen,*
Rådhuspladsen, Copenhagen.
Below: *Typical Hot Dog Stand, Copenhagen.*
(Both photos: Norman P.T. Renouf)

Tivoli Christmas Market.
(Norman P.T. Renouf)

Above: *Spiral Steeple, Vor Frelsers Kirke, Christianshavn.*
(Cees van Roeden, Danish Tourist Board)

Below: *Ribe Cathedral.*
(Ole Arkhøj, Danish Tourist Board)

Neptune Fountain, Frederiksborg Castle, Hillerød.
(Bob Krist, Danish Tourist Board)

Above: *Interior, Royal Museum of Fine Arts, Copenhagen.*
(Jørgen Schytte, Danish Tourist Board)

Below: *Tivoli, Main Entrance.*
(Jreneusz Cyranek, Danish Tourist Board)

Above: *Nyhavn Canal, Copenhagen.*
(Per Sohlberg, Danish Tourist Board)

Below: *National Gallery, Copenhagen.*
(Jørgen Schytte, Danish Tourist Board)

Above: *House in Christiania, Copenhagen.*
(Bent Næsby, Danish Tourist Board)

Below: *Cycle Taxi.*
(Jreneusz Cyranek, Danish Tourist Board)

Above: *Strædet (Pedestrian Street), Copenhagen.*
(Ole Akhøj, Danish Tourist Board)

Below: *Cruise Ship at Night, Langelinie.*
(Jørgen Schytte, Danish Tourist Board)

Above: *A Gala Evening at the Old Børsen.*
(Cees van Roeden, Danish Tourist Board)

Below: *Rundetårn (The Round Tower).*
(Jørgen Schytte, Danish Tourist Board)

Rosenborg Slot & Kongens Have, Copenhagen.
(Jreneusz Cyranek, Danish Tourist Board)

Above: *Palace Guard at Amalienborg Plads.*
(Jørgen Schytte, Danish Tourist Board)

Below: *Christiansborg Riding Grounds.*
(Nicolai Perjesi, Danish Tourist Board)

Above: *Thatched Holiday Cottage.*
(John Sommer, Danish Tourist Board)

Below: *Wood Anemones*
(Wedigo Ferchland, Danish Tourist Board)

Roskilde Cathedral with Snow.
(Søren Lauridsen, Danish Tourist Board)

Above: *Louisiana Museum of Modern Art, Humlbæk.*
(Nicolai Perjesi, Danish Tourist Board)

Below: *Landscape on Roskilde Fjord.*
(Søren Lauridsen, Danish Tourist Board)

Above: *Ribe, Slippe.*
(Courtesy of Ribe Tourist Bureau)

Below: *Amagertorv (Strøget), Copenhagen.*
(Courtesy of Danish Tourist Board)

Above: *Øresund Bridge.*
(Jørgen Schytte, Danish Tourist Board)

Below: *Poplars on Funen.*
(Cees van Roeden, Danish Tourist Board)

Houses on Christianshavn Canal.
(Henrik Stenberg, Danish Tourist Board)

Above: *Store Bælt Bridge, Funen.*
(Søren Madsen, Danish Tourist Board)

Below: *Kronborg Castle, Helsingør.*
(Bob Krist, Danish Tourist Board)

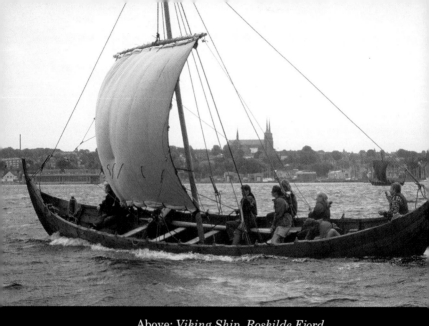

Above: *Viking Ship, Roskilde Fjord.*
(Bob Krist, Danish Tourist Board)

Below: *Girl with Red Balloon.*
(Søren Lauridsen, Danish Tourist Board)

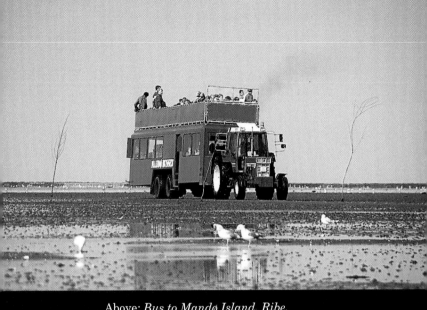

Above: *Bus to Mandø Island, Ribe.*
(Courtesy of Ribe Tourist Bureau)

Below: *Skibbroen, Ribe, at Night.*
(Courtesy of Ribe Tourist Bureau)

Mounted Police Officer, Amagertorv, Copenhagen.
(Søren Lauridsen, Danish Tourist Board)

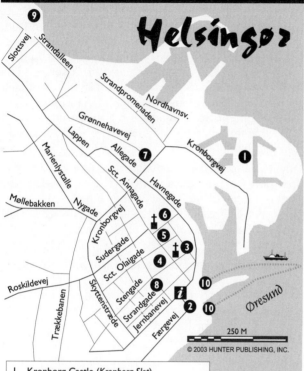

Helsingør

© 2003 HUNTER PUBLISHING, INC.

1. Kronborg Castle (*Kronborg Slot*)
2. Central Station; Tourist Information
3. Saint Olai's Church (*Sct. Olai Kirke*)
4. Town Hall (*Rådhus*)
5. Carmelite House/Town Museum (*Bymuseum*)
6. Saint Mariæ Church (*Sct. Mariæ Kirke*)
7. *Danserindenbønden* (Park)
8. Old Ferry Street (*Gammel Færgestræde*)
9. Casino & Hotel Marienlyst
10. Docks for Ferry to Helsingborg

N

Helsingør

Historic Streets

Turn left and stroll down **Strandgade** to see some
rather attractive wood frame buildings dating from
the 16th century. At that time (long before the railway lines and station were built on reclaimed land),
the houses to the left backed onto the sound. The
house at number 55 dates from 1592. The oldest
wood frame building in Helsingør is at number 17, at
the junction of Strandgade and **Skyttenstræde**; it
is the former home of The Anchor pub, and was constructed in 1577.

Turn right onto Skyttenstræde and, along the way to
Stengade just a block away, take a look at the
quaint, colorful and low-slung houses in **Anna
Queens Stræde** to the left, which paint a scene that
wouldn't have looked out of place centuries ago.

Stengade, undoubtedly, is Helsingør's most popular and busiest shopping street; the array of stores
found along both sides is eclectic indeed. It goes
without saying that many of these survive by selling
alcohol to Swedes, but many have a fine selection of
food and other goodies as well.

Stengade is not without buildings of historical import. Number 20 is the best-preserved timber-frame
house in town. The impressive façade of the **Town
Hall** (*Rådhus*), where Christian IV met with Scottish diplomats in 1589, dates from the mid-16th century. You will also find an element of human entertainment on Stengade, especially on those busy Saturdays. It is amusing simply to watch the shoppers
search for their bargains, and any number of human
statues (a popular form of street performance) will
likely be vying for your money and attention.

Turn the corner now onto **Sct. Anna Gade**, home to
two churches and a museum, as well as a host of little shops and a restaurant or two to entice you.

Historic Churches

Although the overall street plan of Helsingør dates from the early 15th century – the time of Erik of Pomerania – the **Church of Saint Olai** (*Sct. Olai Kirke*) was here well before that period. It was consecrated around the beginning of the 13th century; the imposing, but rather irregular, present-day façade arose between 1480 and 1559. Since 1961, it has functioned as Helsingør's cathedral but, long before that, it was the favored last resting place of many of the town's most prominent citizens.

On the same side of the street is **Carmelite House**, an elegant, early 16th-century structure that has had various roles – first as a hospital for foreign sailors, then as a private mansion, then as a poorhouse – and now serves as the **Town Museum** (*Bymuseum*). Its exhibits detail the history of Helsingør, with an emphasis on the Sound Tolls era. The museum is open daily, from midday to 4 pm; ☎ 21-00-98. Directly across from the museum are an antique shop and the **Hotel København**.

Beyond the museum stands a cluster of buildings that are both historically important and architecturally interesting. All but one of these constitute the **Monastery of Our Lady** (*Karmeliterklosterest*), a 15th-century convent of the sober Carmelite order. This is considered to be one of the best-preserved medieval convents in Northern Europe; it boasts a particularly beautiful brick cloister, with arches below and windows above, that stands in lovely contrast to the simplicity of a single tree surrounded by daffodils at its center.

Note the magnificent display of beer mugs in the windows that flank the door of the Hotel København.

In this group of convent buildings is the forceful-looking **Church of St. Mariæ** (*Sct. Mariæ Kirke*). The interior is quite interesting, with frescoes, elaborate boxes once reserved for the use of rich merchants, and two votive ships. Both the church and the convent were constructed around 1430, at the time that the Sound Dues were introduced.

The Reformation in 1536 led to the demise of the church; the buildings were, at one time, even used as an inn. A royal charter in 1573 commanded the church's destruction; it avoided this fate when, in 1576, King Frederick II made a concession to the vast number of foreigners living in Helsingør and allocated it as a church for the German-Dutch community. Services were conducted here in German until the end of the 17th century; by that time the German community had dwindled, and by 1851 all services here were conducted in Danish.

Sct. Anna Gade ends at the much busier and blander Kronborgvej. At the intersection with Allégade, the small **Danserindebønden** park offers a little resting place. You will see larger houses on the left as the road makes a sweeping curve toward the castle to the right; the Sound and the coastline of Sweden appear in the distance. The entrance to the castle is just across from a wet-dock.

To return to the railway station from Kronborgvej, turn left into Allégade and then Havnegade by the Danserindebønden park. This part of the walk won't become interesting until you draw level with the vessels docked alongside the wharf. The railway that parallels the route leads to a station just before the ferry terminal; this is the Helsingør end of the single track **Helsingør-to-Gilleleje** line, operated by HHGB, that runs around the coast. The structures across from here, noticeably larger and more imposing than others in the area, date back to the affluent era of the Sound Dues. Finally, before approaching the station, a peek into the narrow **Old Ferry Street** (*Gammel Færgestræde*) – so named as it once led down to the ferry landing – will raise your curiosity as to exactly how people actually managed to live here.

Once you have completed your walking tour and your visit to the castle, consider a short (20-minute) ferry trip across the sound to Helsingborg, Sweden (see page 173).

Kronborg Slot

A Brief History

Erik of Pomerania built the first fortification on this spot in the 1420s, naming it Krogen. It was from here that his forces controlled shipping in the Øresund, and exacted the Sound Dues. Between 1574 and 1585, Frederik II, influenced by the architectural and social styles of his era, built a sumptuous Renaissance-style castle on the site. He commissioned the Flemish architect **Antonius van Opbergen** to design the four-wing structure; the new castle was named Kronborg. Various Danish and Dutch artists were then engaged to create painted, woven and sculpted decoration on a scale never before seen in Scandinavia.

In September of 1629, some 40 years after the completion of the castle, a fire destroyed everything except the chapel, and it was left to Christian IV to rebuild. While the exterior was replicated along the original lines, the interior décor of the new castle was distinctly early baroque. Only 30 years later, in September 1658, rampaging Swedes ransacked the castle and left with a valuable haul of expensive treasures. Following completion of the necessary repairs, Christian V wisely directed the enhancement of the outer defensive fortifications in 1690. However, beginning in the late 18th century, Danish royalty lost interest in Kronborg. From that time until 1923, when it was restored to its 16th- and 17th-century appearance, the structure was relegated to use as an army barracks.

Helsingør

A notice board informed visitors that it would take between 20 and 25 years for the typical green patina to appear on the castle's new copper roof.

Kronborg is one of Northern Europe's most important Renaissance castles, and the entrance is intimidating, as it should be. In order to gain the best view, you must first pass over a moat to an island, then pass again over the same moat through the Kronværk gate. It will become apparent from this vantage point that a large scale redevelopment project, planned for completion in 2010, is being undertaken.

Facing you is another moat, this one three-sided, which you follow around the castle walls to reach the main entrance. On the way, you will pass a tunnel that leads to the outer fortifications; these overlook the Øresund, and bear some investigation.

Danish Maritime Museum

Located here since its inception in 1915, this museum offers quite an interesting series of exhibits, among which are model ships and various other artifacts illustrative of the life and work of a sailor. The exhibits are designed to give the visitor a comprehensive understanding of Danish maritime traditions from the 15th century to the present. Occupying most of the first floor of the castle, it also gives glimpse of what you can expect to see when visiting the main halls.

The castle's rather dark and dingy casemates are home to a statue of **Holger Danske**. Apparently, this legendary Danish figure was birthed in medieval France by a heroic verse called *The Song of Roland*, which first appeared in Scandinavia around 1510. A Danish version, *King Olger Danske's Chronicle*, was published around 1534 by local author **Christian Pedersen**, and thus became associated with Kronborg.

The Legend of Holger Danske

Over the centuries, Holger Danske has come to play an important part in the Danish consciousness, to the point where his name was chosen for one of the most important resistance groups during the Nazi occupation. The stone statue seen today is a 1985 copy of the original plaster statue that, unfortunately, succumbed to the dampness of the casemates. It depicts this formidable warrior sleeping, arms crossed over a sword. Legend has it that the moment external enemies threaten Denmark, Holger Danske will turn into flesh and blood and defend the country.

The 1948 film Hamlet, starring Sir Laurence Olivier and Jean Simmons, was shot at Kronborg.

The Story of Hamlet

Helsingør

Holger Danske is not the only mythical figure who is associated with Kronborg. The story of **Amled**, who made his first appearance in literary traditions more than 800 years ago, was brought to the attention of the Danes by Christian Pedersen – the same author who chronicled Holger Danske – in 1514. It is widely believed that this legend, transformed into a story of revenge, was the basis for English playwright William Shakespeare's now-famous tragedy *Hamlet*; it was most likely this play that connected the character to Elsinore (Helsingør) and Kronborg. Since 1816, many stage performances of *Hamlet* have taken place at Kronborg.

The Castle

The main halls are sparsely furnished but, nevertheless, immensely impressive; they evoke impressions of solid strength and royal presence throughout. This is particularly so in the huge, 64 meter by 11 meter (210 ft by 36 ft), oak-beamed **Banqueting Hall**, which is regarded among the most noble rooms of the Danish Renaissance period.

Kronborg's Banqueting Hall is the largest hall of its kind in northern Europe.

Nowadays, its walls are adorned by 12 paintings of the Øresund by Isaac Isaacsz. In the past, these same walls were hung with 42 famous tapestries created by the Dutchman Hans Knieper, depicting the 111 Danish kings said to have reigned before Frederik II. Fourteen of the tapestries still survive, and seven of those are in a small room beneath the hall. The rest are in the **Danish National Museum**, which is at Frederiksborg Slot in Hillerød (see page 155).

The **King's Chamber**, designed by Frederik II in 1576, has a bay window overlooking the ramparts so that he could inspect visitors to the castle. The **Queen's Chamber**, arranged by Frederik II for Queen Sophie of Mecklenberg, allowed her to have direct access through the East Wing to the **Gallery Chapel** and, via a small staircase, to the **Ballroom**. As you move from room to room there are some very detailed and informative leaflets that give visitors a real insight into the history and lifestyle of Danish royalty.

Kronborg Slot dominates the Øresund today, as it was always meant to. Its historical importance is such that, on November 30, 2000, it was added to UNESCO's World Heritage List of significant buildings. For the Danes themselves, though, Kronborg Slot is more than just a beautiful and historic castle; it is a monument of true national significance.

Kronborg, ☎ 21-30-78 or www.ses.dk, is open daily from May to September, 10:30 am to 5 pm; in October and April, hours are Tuesday to Sunday, 11 am to 4 pm; from November to March, hours are 11 am to 3 pm. The sea barriers stay open daily from 6 am to sunset; the Danish Maritime Museum is open during the same hours as the castle. Admission is free to holders of the Copenhagen Card; without the card, admission to all of Kronberg is DKK 60; admission to just the halls, chapel and casemates is DKK

40; and admission to the chapel and casemates only
is DKK 25.

Shop Till You Drop

ABACUS
Brostræde, 1B
☎ 49-26-49-86

There are, of course, numerous tourist shops in Helsingør, but this one is just a little bit different. In a small street very close to the tourist office, this shop is run by Carol and Maria who, between them, speak Danish, English, German, French, Bahasa Malaysia and a smattering of Spanish. They are very attentive to their customers, a thoroughness reflected in the fine array of specialty goods on show in their little shop. These include, among a host of other items, Danish ceramics, hand-blown glass, beautiful dolls, Scottish woolen products, porcelain pillboxes, silk scarves, pewter, and hand-tooled leather goods.

OLE JENSEN APS
Stengade, 19
☎ 48-21-12-18

If you are partial to cheese and other such delicacies, a stop here is essential. And, when you get a craving for more of the same back in Copenhagen, you can visit their shop at Købmagergade, 19 (see page 96).

Festivals

Hamlet Summer, featuring all kinds of cultural, musical and theatrical activities, takes place every August on the waterfront; www.hamletsommer.dk.

The **Helsingør August Jazz Festival** and **Baltic Sail Helsingør**, a maritime festival, also take place in August. For current information, check on-line at www.balticsail.dk, or check with the Helsingør tourist bureau at www.visithelsingor.dk.

After Dark

CASINO MARIENLYST
Hotel Marienlyst
Nordre Strandvej 2
☎ 49-21-49-00, fax 49-21-40-00

The casino's **Dinner & Play** package includes a welcome drink, three-course dinner and coffee in the **Seaside** restaurant, admission to the casino, and cash chips to the value of DKK 200 per person. The cost is DKK 449 per person.

The casino is open 7 pm to 4 am; admission DKK 50. Games include blackjack, Caribbean stud poker, roulette, seven card stud poker and 60 slot machines. Identification such as a passport is required, and minimum age is 18. Dress code is casual.

Best Place To Stay

As Helsingør is so close to Copenhagen, the vast majority of visitors will not contemplate staying here overnight. However, you may want to make Helsingør a base, enabling you to spend time visiting **Helsingborg, Sweden**; the **Louisiana Museum** in Humlbæk; or nearby Hillerød, with its fabulous **Frederiksborg Slot**, which is much closer to Helsingør than to Copenhagen. It would be impractical to try to see the sights of more than one of these destinations on one day-trip from Copenhagen.

HOTEL MARIENLYST ★★★★★
Nordre Strandvej 2
☎ 49-21-40-00, fax 49-21-49-00
www.marienlyst.dk

This modern hotel has a fabulous waterside location. In addition to very nice rooms, amenities include the **Seaside Restaurant**, a nightclub, a pool, and the Casino Marienlyst (see previous page).

Best Place To Eat

THE MADAM SPRUNCK
Stengade 48
☎ 49-26-48-49

This restaurant is in a charming old building in a small alleyway, just off the busy pedestrian shopping street of Stengade. It has a pleasing ambiance and a limited, but somewhat esoteric, menu. One course costs DKK 185, two courses DKK 260 or three courses DKK 315.

Helsingør

Helsingør Information

Emergencies

Ambulance, police and fire . . . . ☎ 112
Medical services . . . . ☎ 48-25-00-41

Tourist Office

HELSINGØR TURISTBUREAU
Havnepladsen, 3
DK-3000 Helsingør
☎ 49-21-13-33, fax 49-21-15-77
www.helsingor.dk, info@helsingorturist.dk

The office, located right by the train station, is open Monday to Friday, 9 am to 4 pm; and Saturday, 10 am to 1 pm.

The **Copenhagen Card** can be purchased here; it is valid for admission to the Kronborg Slot, and also covers train (and bus) transportation between Copenhagen and Helsingør.

Hillerød

A Brief History

Hillerød, prior to 1560, was a simple village. It had grown up around a manor house called Hillerødsholm, which was owned by naval hero Herluf Trolle and his wife Birgitte Gøye. It was awakened from its sleepy existence in short order when King Frederik II took over the manor in 1560 and turned it into a hunting seat, thereby stimulating the growth of the surrounding town. Further expansion followed later in the century when the King, in collaboration with his son – the builder-king Christian IV – began work on a magnificent castle. It was named Frederiksborg in the King's honor.

Hillerød managed to rebound from the triple onslaught of plague, fire and wars with Sweden that befell the town in the late 17th century. But the fortunes of the town, inevitably, have been tied to the fortunes of the castle, and thus, when the royal seat was transferred to the Palace in nearby Fredensborg in the mid-18th century, a serious decline was precipitated in Hillerød. It was not until the 19th century that developing trade, spurred on by the opening of a direct rail line with Copenhagen in 1864, resulted in the emergence of the thriving modern town that you see today.

The City Today

Hillerød is a rather pleasant town with fine shopping, including the award winning Castle Arcades (*SlotsArkaderne*) center built in 1992; an array of public sculptural works; and a number of fine buildings, along with some museums.

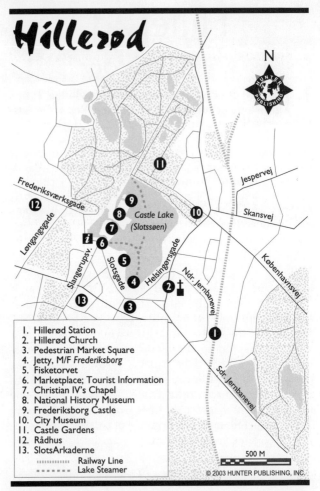

Hillerød

N

1. Hillerød Station
2. Hillerød Church
3. Pedestrian Market Square
4. Jetty, M/F *Frederiksborg*
5. Fisketorvet
6. Marketplace; Tourist Information
7. Christian IV's Chapel
8. National History Museum
9. Frederiksborg Castle
10. City Museum
11. Castle Gardens
12. Rådhus
13. SlotsArkaderne

    ·········· Railway Line
    - - - - - - Lake Steamer

© 2003 HUNTER PUBLISHING, INC.

For most visitors, though, the main attraction is the beautiful Frederiksborg Castle that sits in the lake and is accompanied by fine, newly restored, Baroque Gardens.

Getting Here

By Train

The S-train runs between Copenhagen and Hillerød on a very frequent schedule; in summer, trains depart two or three times every hour on the 30-minute trip. The Hillerød station is about a 10-minute walk from the center of the town; ☎ 48-26-03-65.

Getting Around

By Bus

The number 701 bus takes visitors directly from Hillerød train station to Frederiksborg Slot.

By Boat

The **pleasure steamer** M/F *Frederiksborg* takes visitors to the castle. It's a pleasant stroll from the train station to the lake in the center of Hillerød, where you take the steamer.

During June, July and August the trips are run Monday to Saturday, twice an hour, between 11 am and 5 pm; and on Sunday, between 1 pm and 5 pm. In May and September there are crossings on Saturday, between 11 am and 5 pm; and on Sunday, between 1 pm and 5 pm. The ticket price is DKK 20 for adults, DKK 5 for children.

On Foot

The pleasant walk from the station to the ferry landing or to the castle will take you past most of Hillerød's points of interest, including the pedestrian shopping streets and marketplaces.

Hillerød

Sunup To Sundown

Frederiksborg Castle

History

Although construction of the oldest parts of the castle was begun around 1560 under the direction of Frederik II, the majority of the present-day structure dates from between 1600 and 1620, and was created by Frederik's son, King Christian IV. The castle was built on three islets within the castle lake (*Slotssøen*) in the Dutch Renaissance style, and the result is spectacular.

A boat ride offers a relaxing trip to the castle.

Frederiksborg Castle (*Frederiksborg Slot*) is Denmark's architectural showpiece. It is considered to be Christian IV's grandest achievement and one of the greatest Renaissance castles in northern Europe. This quintessential fairy tale castle, with its sweeping gables, sandstone decorations and copper roofs and spires, was used by the kings of Denmark for over 200 years and, from 1671 to 1840, monarchs were crowned in the castle's chapel. From 1693, the chapel has been used by the knights of the Order of the Elephant and of the Grand Cross of Dannebrog, and to this day it also functions as a parish church.

Fighting fire with beer?

In 1840, however, the royal seat was moved to the new palace at Fredensborg. From that time, the importance of Frederiksborg Castle declined, and years of neglect followed. Adding injury to insult, in 1859 much of the interior was ravaged by fire. Its subsequent restoration was dependent upon private means; funds were donated first by the brewer J.C. Jacobsen, and later by the Carlsberg Foundation, between 1860 and 1884.

Danish Museum of National History

The Carlsberg Foundation financed the interior restoration of Frederiksborg Castle, on the condition that it be turned into a museum; this was done, and the *Nationalhistoriske Museum* was opened in 1878. This is the place to discover over a half-millennium of Danish history. This museum occupies more than 60 rooms of the castle, and has a complete record, in chronological order, of Denmark's history from 1500 through the present.

The beautiful chapel at Frederiksborg – nearly every inch of which is richly carved and ornamented – was the setting for the 1995 wedding of Prince Joachim to Princess Alexandra.

Here, you can learn about the Danish monarchy, beginning with Christian I, who established the Oldenburg line (1448-1863); through all the monarchs of the following Glücksburg line; right down to the present queen. The museum also serves as the national portrait gallery. It contains the country's most important collection of portraits and historical paintings, including those of the royal family from the 16th century forward, and of great Danish personalities; as well as a collection of modern art.

Although the exhibits are important, it is the size and splendor of the the actual rooms of the castle that is most fascinating. The 56-m (185-ft) **Knights' Hall** (*Riddersalen*) is awesome in its dimensions, with tapestry-draped walls, marble floor, and carved wooden ceiling, all reconstructed from old drawings after the 1859 fire.

Hillerød

Christian IV's Chapel

Make sure you visit the chapel (*Slotskirken*) that, somewhat miraculously, escaped the 1859 fire virtually unscathed. Its stunning gilt pillars and high vaulted nave, with fantastically carved wooden ceilings from the reign of Christian IV, are Frederiksborg's ultimate triumph.

Christian IV's chapel was the location of coronations for nearly two centuries. The decoration includes in-set black marble panels engraved with quotes from the scriptures, and marquetry panels in ebony and rare woods. Both its altar and pulpit are fashioned of ebony and embellished with biblical scenes in silver relief. The organ is one of Europe's most notable, an almost unaltered original from 1610 by Flemish master Esaias Compenius. Around the chapel's gallery, the window piers and recesses are hung with coats-of-arms belonging to knights of both the Order of the Elephant and the Order of the Grand Cross of Danneborg.

Frederiksborg Slot, ☎ 26-04-39 or www.slotte.dk, is open daily, April to October, 10 am to 5 pm; and November to March from 11 am to 3 pm. Admission is DKK 45.

The Baroque Gardens

Between 1720 and 1725, Frederick IV oversaw royal architect and landscape designer Johan Cornelius Krieger in the laying out of the Baroque Gardens (*Slotshaven*). The plan of the garden is characterized by a central axis, with the symmetry seen in Italian and French gardens of the era. During a period that spanned about 40 years, Frederik IV and the two monarchs who reigned after him, Christian VI and Frederik V, saw that the gardens were properly maintained. Unfortunately, the succeeding sovereigns, who didn't hold the gardens in such high regard, allowed them to become overgrown. Although, beginning in 1850, there were those who expressed a desire to recreate the gardens, it wasn't until 1993 that the financial backing for doing so was found. Frederiksborg's Baroque Gardens were inaugurated three years later, on June 5th, 1996. Visitors today can enjoy a peaceful stroll among its 65,000 box plants; 166 pyramid-shaped yews; 375 lime trees; and 7,000 hornbeam plants.

The Baroque Gardens at Frederiksborg are overlooked from the castle, but not to be overlooked by visitors.

The Baroque Gardens are open from May to August, 10 am to 9 pm; in September and April, 10 am to 7 pm; in October and March, 10 am to 5 pm; and from November to February, 10 am to 4 pm. Admission is free.

Festivals

The **Hillerød Castle Festival** (*Hillerød Slotsfestival*), which takes place every June, offers **ballet** and **opera** productions in the inner courtyard of Frederiksborg Castle. For schedule and ticket information, contact the Hillerød Tourist Bureau (see next page).

Shop Till You Drop

THE SWEATER HOUSE
Slangerupgade 1
☎ 48-25-51-25 or www.sweaterhouse.dk

A Scandinavian sweater from The Sweater House is a souvenir of choice. This shop is conveniently located in the marketplace just outside the entrance to the castle. In addition to an extensive range of souvenirs, this shop is famous, as its name implies, for carrying one of the largest selections of traditional Scandinavian sweaters available in Denmark. The prices here are very competitive indeed, often quite a bit lower than you would pay in Copenhagen or elsewhere.

Hillerød

Best Place To Eat

A comprehensive investigation of the Frederiksborg Slot will likely find you in Hillerød during either lunch or dinner.

SLOTSHERRENS KRO
☎ 48-26-75-16

Adjacent to the castle, and close to the Baroque Gardens, this restaurant features a large terrace that stretches down to the Castle Lake. In agreeable weather, this makes for a pleasant al fresco dining experience. In the high season, April to October, it is open from 10 am to 9 pm; during the months of March and November it is open from 11 am to 4 pm.

Hillerød Information

Emergencies

Ambulance, police and fire . . . . ☎ 112

Pharmacy

Frederiksborg Apotek, offering 24-hour service, is at Slotsgade 26, ☎ 48-26-56-00.

Tourist Office

HILLERØD TURISTBUREAU
Slangerupgade 2
DK-3400 Hillerød
☎ 48-24-26-26, fax 48-24-26-65
turistbureau@hillkomm.dk, www.hillerodturist.dk

The tourist information office is close to the entrance to Frederiksborg Slot. It is open Monday through Saturday, but hours vary seasonally.

Roskilde

A Brief History

Roskilde, with a history dating back to the Viking Age in the late 10th century, is not the oldest town in the country, although it comes close. It certainly is, though, the most important among the oldest towns. Around AD 1000, following his conversion to Christianity, King Harald Blacktooth built a small wooden church; it is believed to have been upon the site of Roskilde's present cathedral. Thus began a rich heritage of crown and church that was the source of fame and fortune for Roskilde. Shortly thereafter, possibly about 1020, the See of Roskilde was established. This led, in rapid succession, to the establishment of no fewer than 14 parish churches and five convents and monasteries. Indeed, by the Middle Ages, Roskilde, with an estimated population of between 5,000 to 10,000, was one of Northern Europe's most important cities.

Roskilde is just a couple of centuries shy of being the oldest town in Denmark.

In 1413, Queen Margrethe I became the first in a long line of Danish monarchs to be interred in the cathedral. Since that time, 38 kings and queens have been laid to rest within this magnificent church.

The tide of change turned against Roskilde in 1536 with the arrival of the Reformation. Subsequently the Catholic Church, many of the parish churches and all of the convents and monasteries were abolished. These fundamental changes precipitated a decline in the city's fortunes that continued for three centuries.

It wasn't until 1847, when Roskilde's population had dropped to just 1,500, that the opening of the first railway line in Denmark, running between Copenhagen and Roskilde, breathed new life into the city's

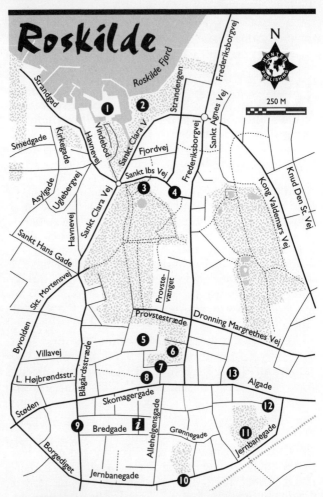

1. Museum Island (*Museumsø*)
2. Viking Ship Museum (*Vikingeskibshallen*)
3. Glassworks Gallery (*Glassgalleriet*)
4. Church of Saint James (*Skt Ibs Kirke*)
5. Cathedral (*Domkirke*)
6. Roskilde Museums
7. Palace Wing, Palace Collections, Museum of Contemporary Art
8. Town Hall (*Rådhus*)
9. Old Shops
10. Central Station; *Vor Frue Kirke*
11. Grey Friars' Churchyard (*Gråbrødrekirkegård*)
12. Horse Market (*Hestetorvet*)
13. Roskilde Priory (*Kloster*)

© 2003 HUNTER PUBLISHING, INC.

fortunes. Since then, building upon its location, Roskilde has transformed itself into a center of commerce and learning, and has capitalized upon its tourism opportunities.

Roskilde has gone from a town of churches to a city of commerce and tourism in the last 150 years.

In addition to its more obvious highlights (the cathedral and Viking Ship Museum), tourists now are attracted in droves to a more modern phenomenon, the **Roskilde Festival** (see page 169).

Getting Here

By Train

There is frequent S-Train and DSB train service between Copenhagen's Central Station and Roskilde, with a travel time of between 19 and 30 minutes – depending primarily upon the number of stops. In Roskilde, ☎ 46-35-23-48. Elsewhere in Denmark, ☎ 70-13-14-15, www.dsb.dk.

Sunup To Sundown

A Stroll Around Roskilde

This tour begins at the train station, which dates from 1847 and is the oldest in Denmark. Just outside the station to the right, at the junction of Jernbanegade and Algade, is the **Horse Market** (*Hestetorvet*), which was for many centuries the largest square in Roskilde and the home, since the Middle Ages, of its livestock markets. Take a moment to inspect the three huge urns (each is five m (16 ft) tall and weighs about 24 tons) which are, unfortunately, decorated with graffiti. Created by Peter Brandes and known as the **Roskilde Jars**, these were presented to the city to commemorate its 1,000-year anniversary in 1998.

Roskilde

At the bottom of Hestetorvet, turn left into **Algade**. Formerly a fashionable neighborhood of prosperous merchants' homes, these now have all but disappeared, giving way to a host of stores. Press on past these in the direction of the spires that tower in the distance, where Algade terminates at **Stændertorvet**, a square laid out in 1908.

GREY FRIARS' CHURCHYARD

Looking to your left as you exit the station, you will see what, at first glance, may appear to be a park. It is, in fact, the *Gråbrødre Kirkegårde*. Since the Middle Ages, this has been the burial place for many prominent citizens of Roskilde.

The Market Square

If you are visiting Roskilde on a Wednesday or Saturday before 2 pm, you will be treated to the experience of a traditional bustling market at Stændertorvet. If you are here on a Sunday, look for a lively flea market. Here also you will come face-to-face with the 1884 façade of the **Town Hall** (*Rådhus*), distinguished by those strange, characteristically Danish, stepped-up spires, a clock, and a small bell tower. On the far side of Stændertorvet stands the elegant, pastel colored **Roskilde Palace**, with the cathedral dominating in the background. Both of these merit close inspection, but first take a short detour to the tourist office (*Roskilde-Egnens Turistbureau*), just two short blocks away at number 15 Gullandsstræde.

Check out the small second-hand shop opposite the tourist office.

Follow Bredgade to **Ringstedgade**, where a right turn will lead you to two of Roskilde's most unusual attractions, the Old Grocer's Shop and the Old Butcher's Shop.

SHOPS OF OLD

Brdr. Lützhøfts Købmandsgaard is decorated to recreate how it would have looked in the 1920s, and goods and produce typical of that era are on sale. Ringstedgade 6, ☎ 46-35-00-61. Open Monday to Friday, 11 am to 5 pm; and Saturday, 10 am to 2 pm.

The few products available for purchase at **Slagterbutikken O. Lunds Eftf** are created according to recipes from the 1920s. Ringstedgade 8. Open Saturday, 10 am to 2 pm.

The most interesting route back to the Stændertorvet is by way of **Skomagergade**, the town's main pedestrian shopping street. Once in Stændertorvet, pass through the arch into the courtyard of a pretty baroque building, **Roskilde Palace**, which has figured prominently in Danish history since its construction in 1733. Between 1835 and 1848 it housed the Assembly of the Estates of the Realm for the Islands; in 1849 the new constitution of Denmark was formulated here. Since 1923, it has served as the bishop's palace. Presently, it also houses two museums: the **Museum of Contemporary Art** and **The Palace Collections**, as well as an exhibition area, **The Palace Wing** (see *Museums*, page 168).

The overwhelming presence in this part of Roskilde, as indeed it is in most parts of the town and surrounding countryside, is that of the tall towers with unusually pointed spires. These belong to the **Cathedral** (*Domkirke*), considered to be one of the most remarkable buildings in Denmark (see page 166).

Leave the Cathedral Square (*Domkirke Pladsen*) by way of Skolegade, which initially passes some very pleasant houses and then enters a park, the *By-*

Roskilde

parken. Here, take the pathway leading down toward the water in the distance. At the bottom of the hill, past a children's playground and across a traffic circle at Sankt Clara Vej, is a rather strange looking building that used to house the city's gasworks but these days contains works of a much more elegant kind – a glassworks gallery.

Glassgalleriet is a great place to pick up a unique souvenir of your trip to Roskilde.

Here, you can watch glassblowers at work creating glasses, dishes and vases. You can even purchase an attractive souvenir to take home. The shop is open Monday to Friday, 10 am to 4:30 pm; and Saturday and Sunday, midday to 4:30 pm. **Glassgalleriet**, Sankt Ibs Vej 12, ☎ 46-35-65-36.

A left turn onto Sankt Ibs Vej will bring you to Roskilde Fjord and the city's other main attraction, the **Viking Ship Museum** (*Vikingeskibshallen*). In 1997, after years of planning, the museum opened a harbor complex called the **Museum Island** (*Museumsø*), making this a much more expansive site than it was on the author's first visit to Roskilde, some years back; see page 167 for details about the museum.

To continue the walking tour from Sankt Clara Vej, follow Sankt Ibs Vej to the right along the park, to the ruins of the **Church of St. James** (*Sankt Ibs Kirke*), which dates from around 1100. This church has not had an active congregation since 1808, and has worn several hats since that time. It is open daily, sunup to sundown, from late April to late October.

The route becomes noticeably steeper as you enter Frederiksborgvej, but some attractive houses – particularly those at numbers 3 and 16 – a church, and an old hospital will provide some diversion. The ground then levels out, and the road changes its name to Sankt Ols Gade, where the **Roskilde Museum** is located at numbers 15 and 18 (see page 169).

For the last leg of your tour continue along Sankt Ols Gade, noting, to the right, the low-slung orange houses that are part of the Palace and, on its corner with Algade, the attractively restored façade of the **Hotel Prindsen**. It's now a simple matter of following Algade to the left, turning right into Hestetorvet, and walking up to the railway station. As you walk along Algade, note the very attractive building that sits back at the end of a small park. This is the **Roskilde Priory**. Built in 1560 as a private mansion, it became, in 1699, the first home for unmarried noble ladies in Denmark.

The Cathedral

Despite its exterior being more austere than attractive, this cathedral is considered one of the most remarkable buildings in Denmark, and is on UNESCO's World Heritage List.

The origins of this cathedral (*Domkirke*) are humble. King Harald's original small church was replaced, in the 1170s, with a brick and stone cathedral constructed at the direction of Bishop Absalon, the founder of Copenhagen. During the course of the next 300 years, the cathedral evolved into a Romanesque-Gothic monument, to which Christian IV added the distinctive spires in 1635. Its interior is dramatic indeed; uniquely styled chapels, ranging from the simplest to the most extravagant, are filled with some of the most amazing sarcophagi you are ever likely to see. The floors are covered in tombs, and there is an impressive array of art pieces and religious memorabilia; some of the items are more than a little weird. Such a monumental collection could only spring from the treasures of royalty. Nearly all of the Danish kings and queens subsequent to Queen Margrethe I's interment in 1413 – a total of 38 – are buried here.

On a less somber note, don't miss the curious clock set high on the southwest wall of the nave. As each hour arrives, St. George rears up upon his horse, eliciting a shrill cry from a dragon that lies beneath them. Then, in celebration of the conquest, a female

Roskilde

figure strikes a little bell four times with a hammer and a male figure strikes his bell once.

Exhibits in the **Cathedral Museum**, which is in the Great Hall above the Magi Chapel, detail the 800-year history of the church. Among its more popular items is a copy of a golden dress worn by Queen Margrethe I. Unfortunately, though, the museum has an extremely complicated set of opening hours; it's best to check the current schedule upon your arrival. ☎ 46-35-27-00, or www.roskildedomkirke.dk.

The cathedral itself is open almost daily, year-round, but it is occasionally closed for religious ceremonies, often on Saturday afternoons; check upon arrival. Admission is DKK 12. Guided tours of the cathedral are available from the end of June to the middle of August, in Danish, English or German, at a cost of DKK 30. Tours are scheduled Monday to Friday, at 11:30 am and 1:30 pm; Saturday, at 11 am; and Sunday, at 1:30 pm.

The Viking Ship Museum

The ancient Danes, of course, are renowned for their exploits aboard the Viking ships. It was in the 11th century, when the Norwegians were rampaging through the country, that the Danes actually sank five of their own vessels across a narrow neck of the shallow Roskilde Fjord in order to block the sea route to the town. These vessels lay undisturbed for some 900 years until, in 1962, they were salvaged to become the primary exhibits in the Viking Ship Museum (*Vikingeskibshallen*). The framework of each vessel was reconstructed using metal strips; then the thousands of pieces of wood were treated with preservatives and fitted together in their proper places.

The museum's design, with the water-facing side entirely of glass, gives the illusion of bringing the waters of the fjord almost into the exhibition hall. The museum is lavishly illustrated with photographs and charts; a film, recounting in English the full story of the salvage, is shown in the cinema-cellar.

A newer attraction at the Viking Ship Museum, opened in 1997 after years of planning, is a harbor complex called the **Museum Island** (*Museumsø*). Here you will see craftsmen, using traditional methods, actually building replicas of the Viking ships.

See how they did things in the really old days at Museum Island; Leif Erickson would be proud.

What's more, during the summer months, visitors have the option of booking one-hour sailings aboard one of the replica ships. Finally, if all this adventure whips up a Leif Erickson-sized appetite, the **Restaurant Snekken** at the museum serves lunch, afternoon coffee, dinner, and your favorite beverages in a pleasant ambiance overlooking the water (see page 171).

The Viking Museum and the Museum Island are open May to September, daily, 9 am to 5 pm (admission DKK 52); and October to April, daily, 10 am to 4 pm (admission DKK 43). ☎ 46-30-02-00, fax 46-32-21-15.

Museums

MUSEUM OF CONTEMPORARY ART
(*Museet for Samtidskunst*)
Stændertorvet 3D
☎ 46-36-88-74

This museum has revolving exhibitions of modern art along with performances of modern dance and concerts, films and video and audio presentations. It is open Tuesday to Friday from 11 am to 5 pm; and Saturday and Sunday from midday to 4 pm. Admission is DKK 20, free on Wednesday.

Roskilde

THE PALACE COLLECTIONS
(Palæsamlingerne)
Stændertorvet 3D
☎ 46-35-78-00

During the 18th and 19th centuries, Roskilde was home to wealthy merchants, and items owned by these families, including paintings and household possessions, are exhibited here. Open mid-May to mid-September daily from 11 am to 4 pm; and the rest of the year on Saturday and Sunday from 2 pm to 4 pm. Admission is DKK 25.

THE PALACE WING
(Palæfløjen)
Stændertorvet 3D
☎ 46-32-14-70

In summer, the Palace Wing gardens become an outdoor gallery.

The **Roskilde Art Society** organizes art exhibitions here throughout the year and, during the summer, arranges for sculptural exhibitions in the gardens. The Palace Wing is open Tuesday to Sunday from midday to 4 pm. Admission is free.

ROSKILDE MUSEUM
Sankt Ols Gade 15 & 18
☎ 46-36-60-44

The buildings comprising this museum are attractive in themselves. The well-laid-out exhibits detail the history of Roskilde, Denmark's first capital, from the time of King Harald Blacktooth through successive ages and cultures – up to and including the Roskilde Festival. Open daily from 11 am to 6 pm. Admission is DKK 25.

The Roskilde Festival

This event, which celebrated its 31st anniversary in 2001, is now considered to be one of Northern Europe's most important festivals. It takes place at the end of June and beginning of July; www.roskilde-festival.dk.

Best Place To Stay

Given Roskilde's proximity to Copenhagen, just 25 minutes away, it is unlikely you will be stopping overnight. However, if you do, the following is a good place to stay. The stars reflect the **HORESTA** rating system (see page 10).

HOTEL PRINDSEN ★★★★
Algade 13
☎ 46-35-80-10 or www.hotelprindsen.dk
Seven rooms

The Hotel Prindsen is easily distinguishable by its lovely façade and outdoor terrace. Founded in 1695, this is right in the center of town – just two minutes from the cathedral. The rooms have been upgraded to include all modern facilities, and guests will also enjoy use of an on-site restaurant and bar, sauna, solarium and spa pool. Doubles from DKK 950 to DKK 1,295.

Best Places To Eat

RESTAURANT RAADHUSKÆLDEREN
Stændertorvet
Fondens Bro
☎ 46-36-01-00

This restaurant is in a space that had it origins as a wine cellar as far back as 1518. In those early days, it was run by Roskilde's mayors, magistrates and justices, who sold wine and German beer as a way of raising extra revenue for the city. For 464 succeeding years it was used as a storage area for the city's archives until, in 1982, Roskilde authorities allowed its conversion to a restaurant. It then took a full year for selected craftsmen to restore the structure to its original appearance. These days, it serves up fine cuisine and wines in a warm, authentic ambiance.

Restaurant Snekken is an ideal place to stop and take a break during your walk around Roskilde.

RESTAURANT SNEKKEN
Museumsøen
Vindeboder 16
☎ 46-35-98-16

A thoroughly modern combination of café, brasserie and restaurant, Restaurant Snekken is in the Viking Ship Museum, overlooking the water. It is open daily for lunch, afternoon coffee and dinner.

Roskilde Information

Pharmacies

Dom Apoteket, Algade 52 . . . . ☎ 46-32-32-77
Svane Apoteket, Skomagergade 12 . . . ☎ 46-32-23-00

Tourist Office

ROSKILDE-EGNENS TURISTBUREAU
Gullandsstræde 15
Postboks 637, DK-4000 Roskilde
☎ 46-35-27-00, fax 46-35-14-74
www.destination-roskilde.dk or www.roskilde.dk, info@destination-roskilde.dk

The tourist office is close to the City Hall. Hours vary seasonally, but they are generally there on weekdays after 9 am and weekends after 10 am. The **Copenhagen Card** can be purchase here if you've arrived without one. An alternative, the **Roskilde Card**, is good for all the attractions listed, and is valid for seven days at a cost of DKK 110.

Helsingborg
A Brief History

Helsingborg – on the Swedish coast at the narrowest part of the Öresund – is just four km (2½ miles) from its Danish cousin Helsingør. The city's history can be traced back to May 21, 1085, when it was named in a deed of gift from the Danish king Canute the Holy (Canute IV).

At that time there was just a simple wooden fortification on the hill known as *Landborgen*. In the 12th century that was replaced by a fortress, and later by an even stronger, larger castle.

Danish Origins

In those days, Helsingborg (under Danish control as were her sister provinces of northern Skåne) was an important military and administrative base for the region. During the Reformation in the 16th century, however, there was a marked decline in the city's fortunes, and almost all of the churches and monasteries were destroyed. Even the mighty castle became vulnerable.

Wars With Denmark

Helsingborg's vulnerability continued well into the 17th century. During this time, Denmark and Sweden were often at war with each other. During the **Skåne War**, from 1675 to 1679, most of the city was destroyed, with only **St. Mary's Church**, **Jacob Hansen's House** and the castle's **Kärnan Tower** surviving. Sweden's long struggle to extract its lands from Danish control finally came to a victorious end following one of the bloodiest battles ever

Helsingborg

N

© 2003 HUNTER PUBLISHING, INC.

[Map of Helsingborg showing streets, numbered locations, harbors, and the Öresund]

Södra Stenbocksgatan

Rektorsgatan
Hälsövägen
Skt. Pedersg.
Kopparmölleg.
Bergaliden
Prins Kristians Gata
Wieselgrensg.
Villatomtsvägen
N. Langvinkelsg.
Slottshagsg.
Södra Storg.
Södergatan
Tycho Brahes Plats
Stortorget
Konsul-perssons Plats
Skt. Jörgens Plats
Järnvägsg.
Pålsgatan
Drottningg.
Kungsgatan
Terminalgatan
Promenade
North Harbor
Inner Harbor
Ocean Terminal
Parapet
Parapet
City Harbor
Sound Terminal
500 M
Öresund

1. Kärnan Tower
2. Terrace Stairs (*Terrasstrapporna*)
3. Castle Gardens (*Slottshagen*)
4. School Museum (*Skolmuseet*) & Medical History Museum
5. New Churchyard (*Nya Kyrkogården*)
6. Old Churchyard (*Gamla Kyrkogården*)
7. Music School
8. Library (*Stadsbiblioteket*)
9. Jacob Jansen House; Saint Mary's Church (*Mariakyrkan*)
10. Central Station; Tourist Information
11. Town Hall Square (*Rådhustorget*)
12. Harbor Square (*Hamntorget*); S/S *Swea* Restaurant
13. Small Boat Harbor (*Småbåtshamn*)
14. State Theater & Concert Hall; Henry Dunkersplads
15. Vikingsberg Art Museum; Landborgen
16. Öresundsparken

🚢 Ferries   P Parking

fought on Swedish soil. In 1710, at Helsingborg, **Magnus Stenbock** defeated the Danes once and for all.

Home rule notwithstanding, Helsingborg was not in healthy shape. Wars and epidemics had decimated the population, which fell to its lowest at around 700 people.

19th & 20th Centuries

It was not until the middle of the 19th century that the coming of the industrial revolution sparked a turn in the city's fortunes. And quite a change it half-century, Helsingborg grew at a faster pace than any other city in Sweden. More recently, the development of new technologies has fueled this prosperity, with Helsingborg now being the dynamic center of the Swedish Öresund.

Today, the city has an interesting ambiance, a mix of old and new enhanced by its links with the sea.

Getting Here

By Boat

Although Helsingborg is a charming and pleasant town, there really is not a great deal of historic interest to see here, and a one-night stay is certainly adequate. However, if you are visiting nearby Helsingør, Denmark, you may wish to take the 15-minute ferry ride across the sound, and experience the cultural differences between the two countries.

Ferries are operated by the **Sundbusserne** line (☎ 48-21-35-45); **Scandlines**, ☎ 33-15-15-15; and **HH Ferries**, ☎ 49-26-01-55, www.hhferries.dk.

Round-The-Sound

If you have time for a more extensive trip, purchase a Round-The-Sound ticket, available in either Denmark or Sweden. This allows you to go from Copenhagen to Malmö, Helsingborg and Helsingør, then back to Copenhagen. You will travel by a combination of ferry, train and hydrofoil. You may begin your journey from any one of those cities and end at the city of origin, with the caveat that you always travel in the same direction. Contact the ferry lines or the railway ticket offices for information.

Sunup To Sundown

A Stroll Around Helsingborg

Begin at the tourist office, located in the modern *Central Stationen* complex by the ferry terminal. Then follow Järnvägsgatan to the left along the harbor, toward the **Town Hall** (*Rådhuset*), without any doubt the most impressive building in Helsingborg.

Completed in 1897, this red brick, neo-Gothic structure has a very elaborate façade indeed. It is dominated by a two-level, 65-m (213.2-ft) bell tower topped by a pointed copper roof. Note, also, the stained glass windows that face Drottninggatan, depicting important events in the history of Helsingborg.

Tours of the Town Hall are not available; however, the town hall bells are rung every day at 9 am, midday, 3, 6 and 9 pm. Time your visit so you can catch the concert; passersby enjoy a real audio treat as the bells play enchanting melodies. Stortorget, ☎ 42-10-5-00.

Continue along Drottninggatan, making a short detour if you wish to the new marina of Norra Hamnen. Beyond the marina is **St. Jörgens Plats**, a pleasant little park graced by a fountain that features three prancing nudes. Across the road you will notice the new **Concert House** and **State Theatre**. Past the park to the right, along Hälsovägen, is the **Vikingsberg's Art Museum** (*Vikingsbergs Konstmuseum*; see page 177).

After your visit to the museum, retrace your steps along Hälsovägen, then make a left onto Fägelsängsgaten, home to a variety of new apartments, houses and small stores. The street name soon changes to *Norra Storgatan* (North Storgatan); be on the lookout for a beautiful red brick, wood-framed house at number 21. This is the **Jacob Jansen House**; it is one of only three buildings left standing in the town following the devastation of the 1675-1679 war, and only a few buildings of its genre still exist throughout the Skåne. A restoration of the house was undertaken in 1930-1931. Now owned by the city, it is used for a variety of events.

A little farther along, at Springpostgränden 3, there is a small **sports museum** dedicated to the athletic achievements of people from Helsingborg.

At the point where Norra Storgatan becomes Södra Storgatan is a street called Stortorget; turn left and you will see a flight of elaborate steps, the **Terrace Stairs** (*Terrasstrapporna*), which were inaugurated in 1903 by King Oscar II. These lead up to two round towers connected by two arches, surrounded by a park. If you don't fancy taking the steps, then there is a small elevator that will whisk you to the top of the tower for a mere SEK 10. Whether you climb or ride, you will be rewarded with fantastic views of Denmark across the sound.

A short walk through the park brings you to the tower of **Kärnan** (see below). Beyond the tower, a pleasant stroll leads, in succession, past an open-air theater, a duck pond, a fountain and formal gardens, and brings you to two unusual museums – the **School Museum** (*Skolmuseet*) and the **Medical History Museum** (*Medicinhistoriska Museet*; see pages 177-178).

After you descend the Terrace Stairs back to Stortorget, a left turn onto *Södra Storgatan* (South Storgatan) will take you to **St. Mary's Church** (*Maria-kyrkan*, see page 176). If you happen to visit the church on a Saturday morning in the summer you will most probably find a small flea market in the gardens outside the church; you may also discover that the surrounding streets are full of interesting and eclectic shopping possibilities.

The Castle

KÄRNAN
☎ 42-10-59-91

Kärnan was construced in the 14th century as a replacement for a 12th century fortification that stood nearby. It is an impressive 35 m (114.8 ft) tall with walls 4.5 m (14.75 ft) thick. Kärnan was later integrated into the Helsingborg Castle complex, which stood as a symbol of Danish control over Skåne.

Kärnan Tower is among Sweden's most famous buildings.

Following the Roskilde peace treaty of 1658, the region – and the tower – were ceded to Sweden. Denmark reclaimed it in 1676; Kärnan finally reverted to Swedish control in 1710 after the battle of Helsingborg.

Unfortunately, the tower is all that remains of the castle complex. Its plain but interesting interior can be visited via a rather precarious-looking set of wooden steps. The tower is open from June to August, 10 am to 7 pm; in April, May and September, 9 am to 4 pm; and from October to March, 10 am to 3 pm.

The Church

ST. MARY'S CHURCH
(*Mariakyrkan*)
Södra Storgatan
☎ 42-37-28-30

This exceptional, three-naved example of Danish Gothic architecture was built in the early 14th century, on the site of a 12th-century Romanesque church; the present structure incorporates sandstone blocks from the earlier building. Construction of St. Mary's was finally completed in about the middle of the 15th century; the church's distinctive, steeply gabled tower was not added until the 16th century. The interior is surprisingly modern in style, shunning the plainness of design adopted by most Scandinavian churches.

Mariakyrkan is notable for its elaborate altar, beautiful pulpit, lovely chandeliers and, of course, hanging votive ships, one of which was donated by a ferryman in 1739.

Museums

VIKINGSBERG'S ART MUSEUM
(*Vikingsbergs Konstmuseum*)
Landborgen
☎ 42-10-59-88

The Art Museum is located high on the Landborgen (hill). The museum has a permanent collection of works by famous Swedish artists. Open May to August, Tuesday to Sunday, 11 am to 4 pm; and the remainder of the year from midday to 4 pm, except on Tuesday, when the closing hour is 6 pm.

SCHOOL MUSEUM
(*Skolmuseet*)
Begaliden 24
☎ 42-10-71-80

The Skolmuseet teaches about teaching. It is in the **Östra Skolan**, an old schoolhouse. For those interested in the subject, it details the development of the pedagogic education methods in used in Helsingborg's schools. Open Monday to Friday from 10 am to 3 pm.

MEDICAL HISTORY MUSEUM
(*Medicinhistoriska Museet*)
Bergaliden 20
☎ 42-10-12-79

*Many things
medical, but no
doctor, in this
house.*

This museum is just along Bergaliden from the School Museum, in a building that formerly housed the Children's Hospital. A 1986 renovation restored this impressive late 19th-century building to its original condition. The museum opened to the public in that same year.

Exhibits include medical equipment, furniture, and the like, dating from the early 1900s. The museum is open Tuesday, Wednesday and Thursday, 11 am to 3 pm; and Saturday, 1 pm to 3 pm. Admission is SEK 10.

Best Place To Stay

RADISSON SAS GRAND HOTEL
Stortorget 8
☎ 42-380-400, fax 42-380-404
www.radisson.com
116 rooms

This, one of Sweden's classic hotels, is in the heart of Helsingborg, just a few minutes walk from the harbor. The rooms and suites, some of which are designed especially for female guests, blend old world character with modern décor. The hotel has two restaurants, a bar and separate men's and women's saunas. Double, SEK 1,000.

Best Place To Eat

RESTAURANG S/S *SWEA*
Hamntorget
☎ 42-131-516

As its name indicates, this is a floating restaurant aboard a charming vessel which dates from 1954; it is now permanently moored in Helsingborg's inner harbor. Sit out on deck and select from an impressive array of seafood and meat dishes, and tremendously tempting desserts. Open daily from 11:30 am to 2 am.

Helsingborg Information

Tourist Office

HELSINGBORGS TURISTBYRÅ
Stortorget/Södra Storgatan 1
☎ 42-10-43-50, fax 42-10-43-55
www.visit.helsingborg.se
turistbyrän@helsingborg.se

From September 1 to April 30, the tourist office is open Monday to Friday, 9 am to 6 pm; and Saturday, 10 am to 2 pm. In May, hours are Monday to Friday, 9 am to 6 pm; and Saturday and Sunday, 10 am to 2 pm. In June, July and August, hours are Monday to Friday, 9 am to 8 pm; and Saturday and Sunday, 9 am to 5 pm.

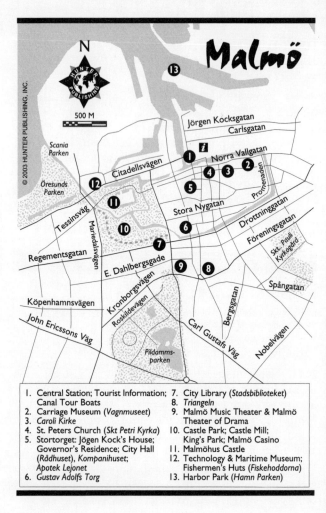

Malmö

500 M

Jörgen Kocksgatan
Carlsgatan

Scania Parken

Öresunds Parken

Citadellsvägen

Norra Vallgatan

Promenaden

Stora Nygatan

Drottninggatan

Föreningsgatan

Skt. Pauli Kyrkogård

Tessinsväg

Mariedalsvägen

Regementsgatan

E. Dahlbergsgade

Kronborgsvägen

Spångatan

Köpenhamnsvägen

Roskildevägen

Bergsgatan

John Ericssons Väg

Carl Gustafs Väg

Nobelvägen

Pildamms-parken

© 2003 HUNTER PUBLISHING, INC.

1. Central Station; Tourist Information; Canal Tour Boats
2. Carriage Museum (*Vagnmuseet*)
3. *Caroli Kirke*
4. St. Peters Church (*Skt Petri Kyrka*)
5. Stortorget: Jögen Kock's House; Governor's Residence; City Hall (*Rådhuset*), *Kompanihuset*; *Apotek Lejonet*
6. *Gustav Adolfs Torg*
7. City Library (*Stadsbiblioteket*)
8. *Triangeln*
9. Malmö Music Theater & Malmö Theater of Drama
10. Castle Park; Castle Mill; King's Park; Malmö Casino
11. Malmöhus Castle
12. Technology & Maritime Museum; Fishermen's Huts (*Fiskehoddorna*)
13. Harbor Park (*Hamn Parken*)

Malmö
A Brief History

Archaeologists and historians have determined that the first inhabitants of this region arrived during the Stone Age – some 11,000 years ago. However, the first written record of Malmö is in a manuscript originating from around AD 1170. The town is again mentioned in church records a century later.

14th & 15th Centuries

Although governed by the Danes for much of its early history, there was a considerable German influence in the region. Evidence of this influence can be seen in the structure of Malmö's **St. Peter's Church**. In 1353, during a brief period of Swedish rule, King Magnus Eriksson granted the city its first charter. A few years later, in 1360, when the Danes again ruled, King Valdemar Atterdag granted a new, but similar, charter.

Erik of Pomerania, crowned as king of the **Nordic Union of Kalmar** in 1397, brought important changes to Malmö and other towns on both sides of the sound by fortifying them; his intent was to limit the influence of the Hanseatic League in this part of the Baltic. Erik built a fortress in Malmö that was quite different in style from the usual local fortifications. Those, like Kärnan in Helsingborg, generally consisted of a single great tower. Erik's preference was to have a fortress guarded by a walled courtyard.

Erik was also responsible for granting the city its coat of arms in 1437; this showed a red-necked griffin with a golden crown. Although modernized recently, the city's emblem is still similar to the original design.

It is thought that the word Malmö drives from Malmhuagar, meaning gravel piles.

16th To 18th Centuries

In the next couple of centuries, Malmö became an important commercial center, with the main product being salt herring – of which as many as 30,000 barrels were exported each year. In this era, too, Malmö held the right to mint the currency of Denmark. The Master of the Mint was a position of great importance. The last – and most famous – person to hold this prestigious job was Jögen Kock, and his house can be seen today in Stortorget.

In 1524 the Reformation arrived in Malmö. The Malmö Treaty, signed by Frederik I and Sweden's King Vasa in that year, stipulated that disputes between the two were to be settled by the German Baltic towns through arbitration. Malmö – and other areas of Skåne – remained under Danish rule until King Karl X Gustav of Sweden defeated the Danes in 1658.

In 1712 an outbreak of the plague decimated the population of Malmö.

The Roskilde Peace Treaty of 1658 ceded the area back to Sweden, and allowed for self-administration in the region. However, the central government abolished this right in 1720, and it wasn't until 1999 that Skåne regained the right to have its own parliament.

The City Today

The industrial revolution of the mid- to late-19th century brought new industries to Malmö, including shipyards, which retained their importance until the middle of the 20th century. During this era, it became Sweden's third largest city, and Malmö's population had grown to over a quarter of a million people by the end of the 20th century.

Getting Here

By Train

In July 2000, the new **Öresund Bridge** complex opened, linking Malmö to Copenhagen and Sweden to Denmark.

The trip from Copenhagen airport (*Kastrup*) to Malmö *Central Stationen* takes just 22 minutes. From Central Station in Copenhagen to Malmö, the trip takes 35 minutes; ☎ 70-13-14-15, www.dsb.dk.

By Boat

The large hydrofoil vessels that make the 45-minute crossing to and from Copenhagen are docked just a few minutes walk from the town center. The one-way fare from Copenhagen is approximately DKK 52, with a 10% discount for Copenhagen Card holders. For reservations, call Scandlines at ☎ 33-15-15-15 (in Denmark), or www.scandlines.dk.

Round-The-Sound

Malmö is one of the cities on the Round-The-Sound route; check with the **railway** or **ferry** authorities listed above, or the **tourist information office** (page 191), for details.

Sunup To Sundown

A Stroll Around Malmö

Start at the **tourist office**, where you can pick up any additional information you may need about Malmö. The office is conveniently located in the **Central Railway Station** (*Central Stationen*).

Malmö

This part of the inner harbor area is surrounded by canals leading to the outer harbor. Leaving the Central Station, you will cross a pedestrian bridge and turn left into **Norra Vallgatan**.

The Old Town

Look for a gear and chain on either side of the name on the Sunnesson building.

As you walk along Norra Vallgatan there are some impressive buildings on the right; note especially the red brick one at number 34 that dates from 1898, and bears the proud name of **Wilhelm Sunnesson & Co.**

On the banks of the canal, you will likely see rowers and fishermen. After a couple of blocks, you come to the **St. Gertrud District**. This consists of 19 structures, all dating from the 16th to 19th centuries, that have been wonderfully restored.

Next, make a right onto **Drottningtorget**, where you will see the **Carriage Museum** (*Vagnmuseet*, see page 189) on the corner. Note the (now non-functioning) water pump in the square.

Östergatan runs from Drottningtorget back to the center of town. Along the way, on the left hand side, are two handsome wood frame buildings. The first of these, **Diedenska Huset**, dates from 1620 and the next, **Thottska Huset**, was built in 1558 and is Malmö's oldest half-timbered house.

Just a little farther along is the red brick outline of the **Caroli Kyrka** with its tall copper spire. Some blocks later it is impossible not to miss, on the left hand side of Östergatan, the magnificent silhouette of Malmö's most impressive church.

St. Peter's Church

St. Petri Kyrka was probably founded at the beginning of the 14th century; it was first mentioned in 1346, when it had already been consecrated. Unfortunately, but typically, most of its original decorations were covered up or destroyed during the Reformation of the early 16th century, and the resplendent décor you see today is of a later date. The tower was added in the late 19th century. St. Peter's is open Monday to Friday, 8 am to 6 pm; and Saturday and Sunday, 10 am to 6 pm.

Stortorget & The Historic District

Just a block away, along **Kyrkogatan**, is Malmö's most magnificent and oldest square, home to a whole host of attractions. Surrounding a huge equestrian statue and a modernistic fountain, you will find the white façade of the **Governor's Residence** (*Residenset*), which was built in 1730; and the even more impressive **City Hall** (*Rådhuset*), which was originally constructed in 1546. The latter was renovated in the middle of the 19th century. It has an ornate balcony supported by six columns and various statues.

Behind City Hall, on a side street, is an even older building, the **Kompanihuset**, a much plainer red brick structure that dates from around 1520. This was once owned by the Danish Trading Company. To reach it, you pass a thoroughly modern concrete-and-glass bell tower.

Leave Stortorget by way of **Sodergatan**, whose entrance is enlivened by five cast-iron band members in a line. This pedestrian street is home to an eclectic array of stores, bars and restaurants – **Harry's Pub Casino** is one – and an impressive old warehouse in the Dutch Renaissance style from the late 16th century. Soon, Sodergatan opens up into another large square, **Gustav Adolfs Torg**, where you will most probably find a fruit and vegetable market in the center (and, perhaps not surprisingly, McDonalds and Burger King), and five fountains along one side.

In Stortorget, almost next to City Hall, there is the Apoteket Lejonet, *the city's oldest pharmacy. It first opened in 1571, and its façade, decorated with a golden lion with its paw on the* Apoteket *sign, dates from 1893.*

Behind this square there is a **pedestrian bridge** crossing the canal; take Södra Förstadsgatan, another, rather less upmarket, pedestrian street, to the rather unusually shaped **Triangeln**. This is a convergence of several streets; in the center is a strange fountain with a gold column and three men holding, between them, a boat, house and a bunch of flowers.

A right turn here, onto **Södra Rönneholmsvägen**, brings you to another elaborate fountain; the two buildings to the left, at the junction with Fersensvägatan are the **Malmö Music Theater** and the **Malmö Theater of Drama**.

Fersensvägatan is somewhat blander, but is enhanced at the end by the sight of the red brick **City Library** (*Stadsbiblioteket*), dating from 1900, across Regementsgatan. You will see that it consists of two buildings; the second, inaugurated in 1997, is called the Calendar of Light, due to its modern design featuring glass and sandstone.

Public Gardens

A statue of a nude woman outside the library marks the entrance to two parks. First walk through the **Castle Park** (*Slottsparken*), which was used during the 19th century by the Malmö Household Regiment as a training ground. These days it is much more peaceful; it opened as a public park in 1900, and has wonderful lakes full of ducks and geese. Castle Park is also home to a collection of statues, including the very famous **The Man and Pegasus** (*Människan och Pegasus*), the masterpiece created by Carl Milles in 1950 (copies of which can be found in Stockholm, Sweden and Des Moines, Iowa).

The **Parkbron**, a small bridge, leads to the **King's Park** (*Kungsparken*), which was opened in 1872 and was the first large park in Malmö. The large building that you will see here was once a restaurant; it is now, after renovations were completed in 2001, the **Malmö Casino**.

The Castle Museums

Cross two more bridges, the *Kommendantbron* and the *Slottsmöllebron*, into the **Castle Garden** (*Slottstradgarden*), where you will come face-to-face with a most incongruous sight: the **Castle Windmill** (*Slottsmöllan*). This can be toured, but is only open Tuesday from 6 to 8 pm.

From here, follow the pathway out to Malmöhus-vägen where, to the left, you will see the building that houses the **Technology and Maritime Museum** (*Tekniska och Sjöfartsmuseet*). This is part of the **Malmö Museer** complex, that, although fascinating in its own right, will hold little real interest to visitors taking this tour. That description, though, most certainly doesn't apply to the museums housed in the **Malmöhus Castle** (*Slottet Malmöhus*, next page.

FISHERMEN'S HUTS

If you happen to pass this way in the morning, and it is well worth the effort, then be sure to stop by the red huts (*Fiskehoddorna*) in a street called *Banérkajen*, close to the Technology & Maritime Museum. These date from the late 19th century; they were moved here, their third location, in the 1930s. Beginning at seven o'clock each morning, local citizens arrive to purchase a wide array of seafood.

Before heading back to the station to end the tour, follow Malmöhusvägen over the **Slottsbron** (Castle Bridge) and along Slottsgatan. Make your way through the side streets to **Lilla Torg**. This square, adjacent to Stortorget, has a number of fine examples of half-timbered houses, some of which are now restaurants and specialty stores. This is an interesting area, and quite popular too, especially at night. The square has a double water pump, trees on three corners, 11 lampposts and even an old-fashioned telephone box. In one corner is a fine example of a *Saluhallen*, an indoor market, converted into a trendy eating place.

Canal Boat Tours

RUNDAN
☎ 40-611-74-88

This company has canal boats that will take you on a 45-minute guided sightseeing tour, during which you will learn much more about the history of Malmö. If you are feeling a little hungry, they also have picnic hampers available for purchase. From late April to late June, these sail between 11 am and 4 pm. From late June to late August, they sail between 10 am and 5 pm, and at 8 pm and 9 pm. Between late August and the beginning of October, they sail between midday and 3 pm. Fare is SEK 70.

Malmöhus Castle

Behind a moat and surrounded by gardens, the red brick façade of Malmöhus Castle (*Slottet Malmöhus*) is most impressive indeed, and the low round towers at the ends make for an unusual architectural contrast. The castle, which had been enlarged by King Frederik I in 1524, burned in 1529. King Christian III oversaw the construction of a new castle between 1536 and 1542, and most of what you see today dates from the mid-16th century, when Malmö was still under Danish rule. After Skåne was returned to Swedish rule, the strategic value of the castle declined. It ceased being a military fortress in 1812.

After being used as a prison until 1909, the castle was utilized as housing for the homeless during the First World War. Following the war, the structure underwent a restoration, and was opened as a museum in 1937. During the Second World War it received refugees, and in April 1945, more than 2,000 concentration camp survivors were housed here.

These days, the castle is the home of the *Malmö Museer* (Malmö Museums; see below).

Museums

THE CASTLE MUSEUMS
Malmöhusvägen
www.malmo.se/museer

This complex consists of the **City Museum**, where you can learn about the history of the city, especially the medieval history under both Danish and Swedish rule; the **Art Museum**; and the fascinating **Museum of Natural History**, with its fine displays depicting animals, and an intriguing aquarium and tropicarium. The Malmö Museums are open daily, year round. From June to August, hours are 10 am to 4 pm. From September to May, hours are midday to 4 pm. Admission SEK 40.

CARRIAGE MUSEUM
(*Vagnmuseet*)
Drottningtorget
☎ 40-34-44-38

Located in a very pretty one-story building, which used to be a cavalry house and market hall, there is on display the largest collection of coaches, bicycles and fire engines in Scandinavia. Open Friday 9 am to 4 pm and Saturday between 11 am to 3 pm during July and August. Admission SEK 10.

Best Places To Stay

RADISSON SAS HOTEL MALMÖ
Östergatan10
☎ 40-23-92-00, fax 40-611-28-40
sales.malmo@radisson
224 rooms

The Hotel Malmö is a modern hotel that prides itself on the fact that its well-equipped rooms are among the largest in all Scandinavia. And if you want that little extra service, try the Business Class. The hotel's **Thott's** restaurant resembles a 16th-century half-timbered house, and in the evenings gas lamps enhance the ambiance in the atrium section of the restaurant. The hotel also has a fitness center with a sauna and solarium and massage facilities.

HOTELL TUNNELN
Adelgatan 4
☎ 40-10-16-20, fax 40-10-16-25

This hotel has a fine central location and a great ambiance. Originally dating from 1911, it has been considerably enhanced with renovations, ensuring that no two rooms are alike. Interestingly, the rooms come in four different sizes.

Best Place To Eat

SKEPPSBRON2 BAR & RESTAURANT
Börshuset
☎ 40-30-62-02

This is considered to be one of Malmö's up and coming gourmet restaurants. In its modern dining rooms overlooking the water you will be treated to a tempting array of delicacies, and many might be attracted to its special SEK 370 menu.

Malmö Information

Tourist Office

MALMÖ TURISTBUREAU
Centralstationen, S-211 20, Malmö
☎ 40-34-12-00, fax 40-34-12-09
malmo.turism@malmo.se

The tourist office is in the city's central train station. It is open in June, July and August, Monday to Friday, 9 am to 8 pm; and Saturday and Sunday, 10 am to 5 pm. From September to May, hours are Monday to Friday, 9 am to 5 pm; and Saturday, 10 am to 2 pm.

Malmö

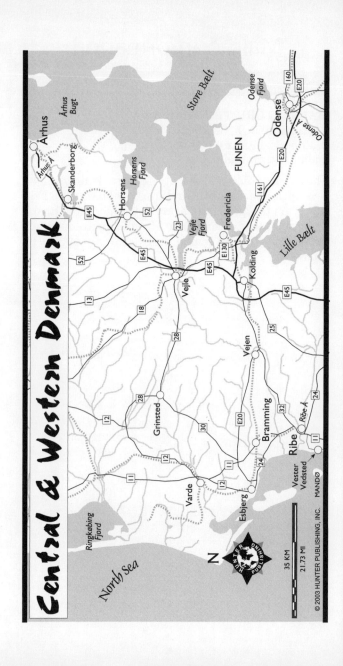

Odense

The city of Odense is on the large island of Funen (*Fyn*), across the Store Bælt, a waterway between the island and western Zealand. Odense is Denmark's only urban borough that is not situated on the coast, though it does have direct access to open water via the Odense River (*Odense Å*) and the Odense Fjord to the north of the city.

A Brief History

Odense, as archaeological finds show, has existed in one form or another for over 4,000 years. Its name, comprised of two Nordic words – *Odins* and *Vi* – translates as Odin's Shrine, a good indication that the warrior god Odin, chief among the Norse gods, was worshipped here in pre-Christian times.

The Vikings erected fortifications on the slopes of the river, the *Odense Å*, to protect the town and control traffic on sea and land. With the introduction of Christianity, Odense evolved into a clerical center; numerous monasteries and churches were constructed in the town.

The earliest known mention of the name Odense was in a letter from the German Emperor Otto III, dated March 18th, AD 988, in which he granted exemption from taxes to the churches of the town, along with those of Schleswig (in what is now Germany), Ribe and Århus. The letter also is evidence that Odense was the seat of a bishopric and, by the standards of the time, was a large town.

In 1086 King Knud IV (Canute the Holy) was murdered by rebellious, tax-burdened subjects in front of the altar of the Church of St. Albans. His remains are interred in the crypt of the cathedral that bears his name – a destination for pilgrimages in the Mid-

Odin is traditionally depicted in the company of wolves; they eat his food, and he consumes only wine. Odin exchanged one eye for a drink from the Well of Wisdom.

dle Ages. During that era, Odense was a dynamic town with many merchants and craftsmen plying their trades.

Even though Odense was the hub of the region of Funen, and has been one of Denmark's largest towns at least since 988, by 1700 it had a scant 4,000 inhabitants and increased its population by only 2,000 over the next 100 years. However, the city grew dramatically in the 19th century. The opening of the railway in 1865 allowed Odense to become one of the country's largest rail junctions; at the same time, a canal was dug from Odense Fjord into the city. The population increased to about 35,000 by 1900.

The City Today

These days, Odense, with a population of 185,000, is the third largest city in Denmark. It is a pleasant city to visit, with a combination of historical places, attractive buildings and parkland. Odense is best known, however, as the birthplace of Hans Christian Andersen.

Getting Here

By Train

The fastest train journey time between Copenhagen and Odense is 1¼ hours, thanks to the relatively new bridge across the *Store Bælt*, the stretch of water between Zealand and Funen. **Odense Banegård Center**, Østre Stationsvej 27, ☎ 70-13-14-15.

Sunup To Sundown

A Stroll Around Odense

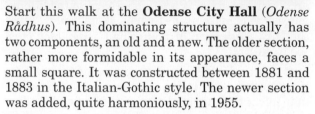

Start this walk at the **Odense City Hall** (*Odense Rådhus*). This dominating structure actually has two components, an old and a new. The older section, rather more formidable in its appearance, faces a small square. It was constructed between 1881 and 1883 in the Italian-Gothic style. The newer section was added, quite harmoniously, in 1955.

Between June 3 and August 29, Monday to Thursday at 2 pm, an hour-long tour is conducted. Beginning at the main entrance, the highlights are the **Wedding Hall**; the **Council Hall**; a **memorial wall**, dedicated to famous residents of Funen who have profoundly influenced Odense; and a **painting** called *Springtime on Funen*. Flakhaven, ☎ 66-13-13-72. Admission DKK 10.

From there, take Vestergade to your right, away from the center of the town. Initially this is a busy shopping street, but that soon changes. You will come to a busy intersection where, towering to your right you will find Sct. Albani, a Roman Catholic church dating from 1908. Cross the street and continue into Overgade, where you will encounter some magnificent examples of timber-framed houses.

A little farther along and on the other side of the street, you will surely be impressed by the colorful and sharp-roofed façade of the **Odense City Museum** (*Bymuseet Møntergården*, see page 200).

At the end of Overgade is a slight diversion. Although the tour calls for a left turn here, take the right turn first to investigate the nearby **Church of Our Lady** (*Vor Frue Kirke*, see page 204). Retracing your steps back to the intersection, continue up Hans Mules Gade, passing the **Police Station** and the **City Hotel Odense** along the way, to the modern Radisson SAS H.C. Andersen Hotel with the **Carl Nielsen Museum** (*Carl Nielsen Museet*) just behind. Across from here, and with a quite different architectural style, is a neighborhood of traditional houses; at Hans Jensens Stræde 37-45, you will find the **H.C. Andersen Museum** (*H.C. Andersen Hus*, see page 199).

Just a little farther down the street is another attraction dedicated to H.C. Andersen, but presented in a clever and unusual way. The **Tinder-Box** is a cultural house for children (*Das Feuerzeug ein Kinderkulturhaus*). In this fairy tale place, children are invited to explore for themselves – through storytelling, drawing, music, and even through acting out their own plays in appropriate period costuming – the world of Hans Christian Andersen. The more grown-up among its visitors will particularly enjoy the very pleasant garden. Hans Jensens Stræde 21, ☎ 66-14-44-11. Open Tuesday to Saturday from 2 pm to 4 pm.

Kings once made this impressive castle their residence when visiting Odense.

Cross the busy **Thomas B. Thriges Gade**, and then make a right along Nørregade to the **St. Hans Church** (*Sct. Hans Kirke*, see page 204). Enter the end of the **King's Garden** (*Kongens Have*); it is dominated by a **castle** (*Odense Slot*) that, unfortunately, is not open to the public.

The dominant building on the opposite corner is the **Odense Theater** (*Odense Teater*). Next door, and equally impressive, stands the **Funen Art Gallery** (*Fyns Kunstmuseum*, see page 200).

Next, make a right at Slotsgade, which is easily recognizable by the First Grand Hotel on the corner, and follow it to Brandts Passage, where you will find three interesting places to stop: the **Art Gallery Brandts Klædefabrik**, the **Museum of Photographic Art**, and the **Danish Museum of Print-**

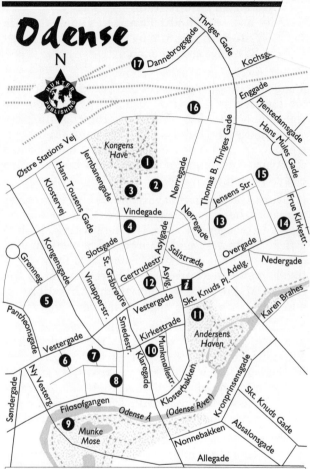

Odense

1. Odense Castle
2. Skt. Hans Kirke
3. Odense Theater
4. Funen Art Gallery
5. Brandts Klædefabrik
6. Brandts Passage
7. Lottrups Gåde
8. City Arcade
9. River Cruise Departures
10. Andersen Childhood Home
11. Skt. Knuds Kirke
12. Post Office (*Lille Gråbrødrestræde*)
13. H.C. Andersens House
14. Odense City Museum; Church of Our Lady (*Vor Frue Kirke*)
15. Casino; Carl Nielsen Museum
16. Central Station
17. Railway Museum (*Jernbanenmuseum*)
.... Railway Lines

NOT TO SCALE   © 2003 HUNTER PUBLISHING, INC.

ing/Danish Press Museum (see page 202). Very close by, also on Brandts Passage, is another, more uniquely interesting museum, the **Time Collection** (*Tidens Samling*, see page 202).

Time for a change of scenery now, so walk to your left along the **shopping street** of Vestergade and look for the narrow entrance to a passageway on the right-hand side. This leads into the charming enclave that is **Lottrups Gård**. This dates from 1791, when Christian Lottrup constructed a four-sided courtyard, consisting of a merchant's home, a corn exchange and stables.

Lottrups Gård was renovated more than once over the years, but it was not until 1984 that it was restored to its original state. It is interesting as a historical landmark, and it provides a peaceful and quiet oasis in the center of the busy city. These days, it is home to an exquisite French restaurant by the name of **Marie Louise**, a florist, and **Alfred Thomsen**, an exclusive pipe, tobacco and wine shop.

Exit Lottrups Gård at the far end, cross the road, and take Filosofhaven down to the much busier **Filosofgangen**. Follow this street to the right, strolling alongside the riverfront park with its running waters and unusual fountains. From here you can cross the footbridge to **Munke Mose**, the departure point for the Odense Aafart river cruises (see page 204).

Retrace your steps now along Filosofgangen, make a left up the slight incline that is Klaregade and a right into **Horstetorvet**. On this street of old, quite small houses which are somewhat incongruously overshadowed by some modern structures, you will find **Hans Andersen's Childhood Home** (*H.C. Andersens Barndomshjem*, see page 200). A short block or so away is the city's magnificent **cathedral** (*Sankt Knuds Kirke*, see page 203). From here, it is just a short stroll back to the Rådhus (City Hall) to end the walk.

Museums

H.C. ANDERSEN MUSEUM
(*H.C. Andersen Hus*)
Hans Jensens Stræde 37-45
☎ 66-14-88-14

This museum, in an attractive area of low-slung pretty houses, is dedicated to the most famous son of Odense. It is considered to be the birthplace of Hans Christian Andersen, a prolific writer who penned 175 well-loved fairy tales and stories, and 14 novels and short stories, as well as numerous plays, travel accounts, poems and biographical works.

Opened in 1908, this is one of the oldest of the museums in the world dedicated to just one author. Numerous artifacts on display depict his lifestyle, and there are many objects collected by Andersen on his travels. Perhaps the most interesting exhibit is the reconstruction of his study in Nyhavn, Copenhagen (the town where he spent his last years), complete with his personal furniture, books and trademark top hat and trunk. Of course, visitors will also find a very large library, filled with over 20,000 editions printed in numerous languages, many illustrations used in those books, and a collection of artwork inspired by his writing. Not unexpectedly, the souvenir shop stocks many of his books, in the language of your choice.

Hans Andersen's works have been translated into more languages than those of any other author!

The H.C. Andersen Museum is open mid-June to August 31, daily from 9 am to 7 pm; the rest of the year on Tuesday to Sunday from 10 am to 4 pm. Admission is DKK 35.

Odense

HANS CHRISTIAN ANDERSEN'S CHILDHOOD HOME

(*H.C. Andersens Barndomshjem*)
Munkemøllestræde 3-5
☎ 66-14-88-14

This branch of the H.C. Andersen museum is housed in his boyhood home. The house where Hans Andersen spent most of his childhood is a diminutive 18 sq m (21.5 sq yards) in size. His family moved here in 1807, when he was two, and lived here until 1819, at which time he was 14. The exhibits trace Andersen's links to his native city. Open mid-June to August 31, daily from 10 am to 4 pm; and the rest of the year, Tuesday to Sunday from 11 am to 3 pm. Admission is DKK 10.

FUNEN ART GALLERY

(*Fyns Kunstmuseum*)
Jernbanegade 13
☎ 66-14-88-14

Funen Art Gallery is in a magnificent building boasting lovely exhibition spaces.

This is one of the oldest art museums in Denmark, with an array of exhibits from the mid-18th century to the present. The special emphasis is on young Funen artists and geometrical abstract art. The establishment of a collection of works by young sculptors is currently underway. There also are regular special exhibitions of both Danish and international art. Open Tuesday to Sunday from 10 am to 4 pm. Admission is DKK 25; higher for special exhibitions.

ODENSE CITY MUSEUM

(*Bymuseet Møntergården*)
Overgade 48
☎ 66-14-88-14

This is a complex of beautiful timber-framed houses that date from the 16th century. They contain a fascinating collection of exhibits detailing life in Odense throughout the ages. The Bymuseet is open

Tuesday to Sunday from 10 am to 4 pm. Admission is DKK 25.

BRANDTS KLÆDEFABRIK
Brandts Passage 37 & 43
☎ 66-13-78-97
www.brandts.dk

This was formerly a large cloth mill; it was among the largest employers in Odense for more than a century. Several years after its closure in 1977 it was renovated to become Denmark's first international center for art and culture, comprised of three museums in one, each with its own opening hours and admission fee. Within this complex you will find three distinctly different artistic experiences.

◆ **Art Gallery Brandts Klædefabrik**

(*Kunsthallen Brandts Klædefabrik*)

Various forms of art, mainly contemporary, are displayed in this museum's three large halls. In July and August it is open daily from 10 am to 7 pm; the rest of the year it is open Tuesday through Sunday from 10 am to 7 pm; closed on Monday. Admission is DKK 30.

◆ **Museum of Photographic Art**

(*Museet for Fotokunst*)

This is the only photography museum in the country that, in addition to its permanent collections, also hosts 10 to 12 temporary exhibitions throughout the year. In July and August it is open daily from 10 am to 5 pm; the rest of the year it is open Tuesday through Sunday from 10 am to 5 pm; closed on Monday. Admission is DKK 25.

Save on admission by purchasing a collective ticket which allows entrance to all three museums at Brandts Klædefabrik.

◆ **Danish Museum of Printing**

(*Grafisk Museum/Dansk Pressemuseum*)

Through a variety of exhibits, the development of the press and printing trades over the last three centuries is detailed. In July and August it is open daily from 10 am to 5 pm; the rest of the year it is open Tuesday through Sunday from 10 am to 5 pm; closed on Monday. Admission DKK 25.

TIME COLLECTION
(*Tidens Samling*)
Brandts Passage 29, 2nd Floor
☎ 66-91-19-42
www.tidenssamling.dk

The Time Collection museum is not handicapped-friendly. It is on the second floor, and there is no elevator.

This museum has an absolutely fascinating collection of exhibits that explore the changes in home interior design, fashion trends and daily life from 1900 up to the 1970s. Open daily from 10 am to 5 pm. Admission is DKK 25.

CARL NIELSEN MUSEUM
(*Carl Nielsen Museet*)
Odense Concert Hall
Claus Bergs Gade 11
☎ 66-14-88-14

Carl Nielsen, who lived from 1865 to 1931, was one of Denmark's most famous composers. His unique style of music is credited with bridging the gap between 19th- and 20th-century styles. This museum was opened in 1988. Quite appropriately, it is housed in a wing of the **Odense Concert Hall**. It vividly portrays the time in which the composer lived.

The Carl Nielsen Museum also has a collection of works by Nielson's sculptress wife, **Anne Marie Carl-Nielsen**, whose work is seen in many cities in Denmark, and reproductions of rooms from the couple's home.

From April 1 to May 31, and from September 1 to October 31, the museum is open Thursday to Sunday, midday to 4 pm; from June 1 to August 31, it is open Tuesday to Sunday, midday to 4 pm; from November 1 to March 31, it is open Thursday and Friday, 4 pm to 8 pm; and Saturday and Sunday, midday to 4 pm. Admission is DKK 25.

Churches

CATHEDRAL
(*Sankt Knuds Kirke*)
Flakhaven
☎ 66-12-03-92

The first church erected on this site was completed at the end of the 11th century; it succumbed to fire in the mid-13th century. By the end of that century, a new and much larger cathedral had taken its place. Further conversions and extensions made in the 16th century produced the style seen today. Inside, take note of the rococo pulpit dating from 1754-1756; the brass and bronze baptismal font from the early 17th century; the oak royal pew; and the triptych altarpiece from the very early 16th century. The latter is considered to be one of the most beautiful Medieval works in Denmark. There are also numerous chapels to view. The inscriptions on the many tombstones read like the *Who's Who* of Odense's most prosperous former citizens.

Sankt Knuds serves as both the parish church in Odense and the cathedral church of the Funen diocese. It is one of the finest examples of high Gothic architecture in Denmark. It is named in honor of King Knud (Canute) IV, who reigned in Denmark from 1080 to 1086 and whose remains, along with those of his brother, Benedikt, rest in the crypt.On April 19th, 1100, Knud was canonized by Pope Paschalis II, making him the first saint in the history of the Danish Catholic church.

The history of the Odense cathedral dates back over 900 years.

The cathedral is open from April 1 to October 24, Monday to Saturday, 9 am to 5 pm; Sunday and holidays, midday to 3 pm. From October 25 to March 31

Odense

it is open Monday to Saturday, 10 am to 4 pm;
Sunday and holidays, midday to 3 pm. It is also open
on December 31 from 10 am to 2 pm.

CHURCH OF OUR LADY
(*Vor Frue Kirke*)
Frue Kirkestræde
☎ 66-12-65-39

A wooden church was erected on this site in the 11th
century; it was replaced by this structure, which is
the oldest church in Odense, dating from the late
13th century. Next to the Church of Our Lady is the
oldest secular building in Odense, built around the
beginning of the 13th century. The church is open
year-round, Monday to Saturday from 10 am to midday.

ST. HANS CHURCH
(*Sct. Hans Kirke*)
Nørregade
☎ 66-12-43-88

This was formerly the abbey church of the order of
St. John of Jerusalem; it is notable for its hatch pul-
pit on the outer wall. It is here that Hans Christian
Andersen was baptized on Easter Monday, 1805.
Open January 2 to December 30, Monday to Satur-
day from 10 am to 4 pm.

River Cruise

From mid-April to mid-October, the boats of
Odense Aafart depart from the pier at Munke
Mose on river cruises. This trip is a real tradition for
locals. In addition to quite pleasant scenery, it is curious to study the Danes, traveling in family groups
or with friends, partaking of this pleasure in the
true Danish spirit – that is, accompanied by crates of
beer.

The Odense Aafart also stops at the **Odense Zoo** (see below), finally mooring at **Fruens Bøge**. From here, if you wish, you can take a short walk to the **Funen Village Open-Air Museum** (see below). If you opt for this side trip, pay close attention to the times of the return sailings, or your visit may be longer than planned.

Expect to be treated to a rousing rendition of a traditional song, Sailing Up The River, that is de rigeur on this trip.

From May 5 to May 31, boats depart at 10 am, 11 am, 1 pm, 2 pm, 3 pm and 5 pm; from June 1 to August 15, departures are on the hour between 10 am and 5 pm; from August 16 to August 31, departures are at 11 am, midday, 2 pm and 5 pm. Contact Odense Aafart at ☎ 66-95-79-96. Ticket prices are DKK 48 with a return; enjoy a 25% discount with the Odense Adventure Pass (see page 212).

Just Outside Odense

Odense

ODENSE ZOO
(*Odense Zoologisk Have*)
Sdr. Boulevard 306
☎ 65-11-13-60
www.odensezoo.dk

The zoo is in the south end of Odense, on the west bank of the Odense Å. Hours vary, with opening time generally at 9 am and closing time between 4 and 7 pm, depending on the season. Admission is DKK 65 to DKK 85.

THE FUNEN OPEN-AIR VILLAGE
(*Den Fynske Landsby*)
Sejerskovvej 20
☎ 66-14-88-14, Ext. 4601

Journey back in time and stroll among 20 buildings dating from the 18th and 19th centuries. Combined, these offer the ambiance of a traditional country village and, what's more, you'll be treated to informative working exhibitions, which give visitors a glimpse of how people farmed in that era.

The museum is open year-round; from April 1 to mid-June, and from mid-August to October 31, hours are Tuesday to Sunday, 10 am to 5 pm. From mid-June to mid-August, it is open daily, 9:30 am to 7 pm. From November 1 to March 31, it is open Sunday and on public holidays, 11 am to 3 pm. Admission is DKK 35.

Shop Till You Drop

Shopping in Odense is concentrated around **Vestergade** and some of the side streets in that area. Most are open weekdays from 10 am to 5:30 pm. Extended seasonal hours and additional days might include Thursday, 10 am to 6 pm; Friday, 10 am to 7 pm; Saturday, 10 am to 2 pm; and the first and last Saturday of each month from 10 am to 4 pm.

INSPIRATION ZINCK
Vestergade 82-84
☎ 66-12-96-93

The ingenuity and beauty of Danish design are world-famous, and this shop offers some of the finest examples in Odense.

Zinck, founded in 1928, has been owned by the same family from that day to the present. Zinck is now affiliated with a group of stores who, together, comprise the Inspiration chain. This store offers such an exciting range of products that, truly, it is difficult to decide where to begin. China, glass and crystal are featured, with such famous names as Royal Copenhagen and Georg Jensen being prominent. There are numerous other items to add a bit of Danish pizzazz to your home, including stylish clocks and barometers and a wide range of attractive and functional cookware. Look, especially, for the remarkably designed weather stations by Jacob Jensen.

ALFRED THOMSEN
Lottrups Gade
Alfred Thomsen's shop is an excellent place to purchase Cuban cigars, including *Cohiba*, *Montecristo* or *Romeo y Juliet* brands. Also on offer is a wide array of fine wines, liquors and champagnes.

After Dark

CASINO ODENSE
Radisson SAS H.C. Andersen Hotel
Claus Bergsgade 7
☎ 66-14-78-10, fax 66-14-78-56

The casino is open from 7 pm to 4 am on weekdays, and from 7 pm to 6 am on weekends; admission is DKK 40. The minimum age is 18, and identification such as a passport is required. Dress code is casual.

Blackjack, four tables; Caribbean stud poker, one table; English roulette, five tables; mini punto banco, one table; video poker, four machines; and 35 slot machines.

Best Places To Stay

The following hotels are listed according to price, with the most expensive first. The stars reflect the **HORESTA** rating system (see page 10). All accept major credit cards unless otherwise noted. Most offer a hearty Danish breakfast, which is usually included in the rate.

RADISSON SAS
H.C. ANDERSEN HOTEL ODENSE ★★★★
Claus Gade 7
☎ 66-14-78-00, fax 66-14-78-90
www.radisson.com
166 rooms

This hotel is in the old part of Odense and, as the name implies, it is close to the H.C. Andersen Museum. Modern in style, inside and out, it has rooms with every expected facility. If you like extras, such as a welcome gift and bathrobes, then request a Business Class room. Doubles from DKK 1,345 to DKK 1,545.

CLARION ODENSE PLAZA ★★★★
Ostre Staionsvej 24
☎ 66-11-77-45, fax 66-14-41-45
www.odenseplaza.dk
68 rooms

A classic structure in its own right, this hotel overlooks the charming Kings Garden (*Kongens Have*). The location is convenient to most attractions; it is a few minutes walk from both the train station and the town center. Enjoy very comfortable over-sized rooms that, like the hotel itself, have an inviting, old-fashioned ambiance. Doubles from DKK 1,250 to DKK 1,550.

FIRST HOTEL GRAND ODENSE ★★★★
Jernbanegade 18
☎ 66-11-71-71, fax 66-14-11-71
www.firsthotels.com
138 rooms

The First Hotel has a classical façade and a location close to the town center and the Arts Museum. Expect well-furnished rooms that come in a variety of sizes, a nice restaurant and bar, and a sauna/solarium. Doubles from DKK 802 to DKK 1,702.

CITY HOTEL ODENSE
Hans Mules Gade 5
☎ 66-12-12-58, fax 66-12-93-64
www.city-hotel-odense.dk
48 rooms

The City Hotel offers very comfortable accommodation at rates that won't break the bank. Built in 1988, it is just on the edge of the city center. If you need a little more space, then it has five luxury two-room hotel apartments in a building adjacent to The Old Inn (see below). Doubles from DKK 895 to DKK 1,495.

BED & BREAKFAST
Ramsherred 17
☎ 66-13-89-36

If you would like the opportunity to stay in a typical Danish home, this offers an inexpensive alternative to a regular hotel. The rooms are pleasant, with color TV, and the hostess is absolutely charming. And it's a real bargain; just DKK 280 for two people sharing a double bed.

Best Places To Eat

DEN GAMLE KRO
Obergade 23
☎ 66-12-14-33

The timber-frame structure that houses this restaurant is considered one of the most beautiful in Denmark. Legitimately dubbed **The Old Inn**, it dates from 1683. Whether you eat in one of the small dining rooms, or in the flower-bedecked, glass-roofed courtyard, the ambiance is enchanting indeed. Expect traditional Danish and French-inspired cuisine, and a menu that changes monthly and features seasonal vegetables.

RESTAURANT ROSENHAVEN
Ostre Stationsvej 24

This gourmet restaurant is in the Clarion Odense Plaza Hotel (see page 209). Like the hotel itself, the ambiance is charming and the service exemplary. The menu is small, but interesting. Expect such unusual delicacies as carpaccio of ostrich thigh, or olive-stuffed coquelet breast. You'll begin your dining experience at this restaurant with a glass of Frozen Red Wine.

A HEREFORD BEEFSTOUW
Vestergade13
☎ 66-12-02-22

Just outside the City Hall, this branch of the steakhouse chain is as delightful as those in Copenhagen and other cities.

Odense Information

Emergencies

Ambulance, police and fire . . . . ☎ 112
Emergency Medical Service . . . . ☎ 66-14-14-33
Daily from 4 pm to 8 am, and weekends and holidays 24 hours a day.

Emergency Dental Service . . . . ☎ 66-11-22-22
Saturdays from 4 to 5 pm; and Sundays and holidays from 10 to 11 am.

Pharmacy

Apoteket Ørnen, Vestergade 80, ☎ 66-12-29-70.

Post Office

Off **Vestergade**, at Lille Gråbrødrestræde.

Tourist Office

ODENSE TURIST BUREAU
Rådhuset, DK-5000, Odense C
☎ 66-12-75-20, fax 66-12-75-86
www.odenseturist.dk, otb@odenseturist.dk

The tourist office is near City Hall. Hours from June 15 to August 31 are Monday to Saturday, 9 am to 7 pm; and Sunday, 10 am to 5 pm. From September 1 to June 14 the office is open Monday to Friday, 9:30 am to 4:30 pm; and Saturday, 10 am to 1 pm.

At the tourist office you can buy the **Odense Adventure Pass**, which costs DKK 100 for 24 hours or DKK 140 for 48 hours. It allows free transportation on city bus, rail and ferry services, and free or discounted admission to all of the attractions listed above.

Odense

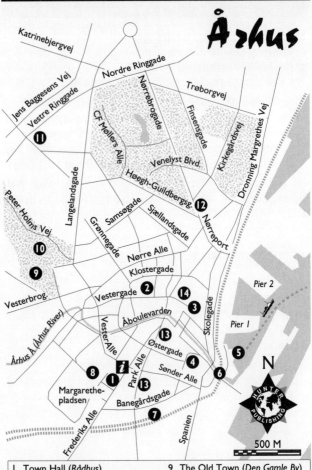

Århus

1. Town Hall (*Rådhus*)
2. Vor Frue Kirke
3. Domkirke, Bispetorvet, Århus Theater, Women's & Occupation Museums
4. Fredenstorv, Fredensgade
5. Ferry Terminal
6. Europa Plads
7. Train Station (*Banegård*)
8. *Musikhus*; Scandinavia Center

9. The Old Town (*Den Gamle By*)
10. Botanical Garden (*Botanisk Have*)
11. Stenomuseum
12. Museum of Fine Arts
13. *Strøget* (Skt. Clemens Torv, Søndergade, Ryesagade)
14. Latin Quarter

i Tourist Information

••••••••••••• Railway Lines
- - - - - - Ferry Lines

© 2003 HUNTER PUBLISHING, INC.

Århus

A port city on the east coast of Jutland, Århus is almost due north of Odense.

A Brief History

Århus, also spelled Aarhus (the two Aa's are equivalent in pronunciation to the one with an accent), was founded by the Vikings. The name is derived from the Old Nordic word *aros,* which translates as "rivermouth." The name was appropriate because the original town, which consisted of a harbor, dwellings and a church, was formed around the mouth of the river. In or about AD 948, a bishopric was established here, with the see becoming permanent in 1060. Another 150 years would pass, however, before the foundation stone of the cathedral was laid in 1201. It was at that time that the city began to slowly expand, as homes were constructed outside of the walls.

The onset of the 14th century brought with it nothing but problems, as a combination of wars and the Black Plague decimated Århus. The disastrous effects of these events were long-term, and Århus did not show signs of a turnaround until the beginning of the 16th century. As the recovery took hold, many beautiful buildings were constructed in the area known now as **The Old Town** (*Den Gamle By*). Growth from that time forward was steady, reaching a crescendo in the 1860s; an extension of the harbor was completed in 1861, and the railway opened the following year. Århus quickly blossomed into an important rail and maritime trading center, with its harbor becoming the second largest in Denmark as well as the biggest employer in the region.

The City Today

These days, Århus is the second largest city in Denmark, boasting an expanding business community and numerous cultural attractions. It is also renowned for its institutions of higher education, and the nearly 30,000 students bring with them a lively ambiance. With a population of 300,000, Århus might be considered the world's smallest big city. Its history and attractions (not least of which is its pleasant location in a green valley, with beaches and woods in easy reach) make Århus is a particularly interesting place to visit.

Getting Here

By Air

Århus Airport (*Århus Lufthavn*) is some 45 minutes north of Århus by bus (fare DKK 55), and has scheduled service from Copenhagen, Gothenburg, Stockholm, Oslo and London. For information about flights to Århus on **Scandinavian Airlines** (**SAS**), **British Airways** or **Finnair,** contact the airport at www.aar.dk, ☎ 45-87-75-70-00.

By Train

The fastest train service from Copenhagen to Århus Central Station takes just under three hours from Copenhagen. DSB, Banegårdspladsen, ☎ 70-13-14-15, www.dsb.dk.

Sunup To Sundown

City Hall & The Waterfront

City Hall (*Rådhus*) is the ideal place from which to begin a tour of Århus. Even though it was constructed over fifty years ago, the building, with its dominating tower, offers a surprisingly futuristic façade.

Those visiting between the middle of June and the first week of September may take advantage of guided tours of the Rådhus and its tower (reached by way of stairs or an elevator), which are offered Monday to Friday, at 11 am, for DKK 10. If, instead, you just want to enjoy the view from the top of the tower, then tours for this are offered at midday and 2 pm, costing DKK 5. City Hall, Rådhuspladsen, ☎ 89-40-20-00.

As you leave Rådhuspladsen, take a look at the **fountain** that features a man and a woman frolicking beneath spouts of water. Walk up the hill to **Sønder Allé**, and follow it down the hill to your right. This is rather a mixed bag of a street, with a motley collection of stores, including a secondhand bookshop, boutiques and antique shops, a smattering of bars and an interesting bakery. Turn left at Fredensgade, easily recognizable by a most impressive building that has a strange glass room at its top. Follow this street around **Fredens Torv** and cross a very busy junction known as **Europa Place**, keeping the large sign saying *KFKDLG* straight in front of you, to reach the quayside.

From here, between the middle of May and the middle of September, the **M/S *Tuno***, a small motor vessel dating from 1965, takes visitors on their choice of two cruises. The shorter trip takes you around the

Århus

harbor; it lasts about an hour, and costs DKK 45. The longer trip is a relaxing voyage that, on a fine day, offers wonderful views of the local forests and beaches as well as a fascinating array of marine bird life; this lasts 2½ hours, traveling to and from the delightful **marina** at Kalovig Badhavn where there is a half-hour stopover. It costs DKK 75.

Cathedral Square

From Europa Place, take a right turn onto **Skole-gade**, where you will find an interesting collection of small pubs and bars – notably the **Casino Bar** – and American-style fast food restaurants. The ambiance changes again suddenly as you come to two very attractive wood-frame structures. The first of these is black and white with green window trim; the other is red with brick latticework. At its end, Skolegade opens up into Bispetorvet. Take a moment to turn to the left and admire the impressive façade of the **Århus Theater**. Inaugurated in 1900, this theater boasts five stages, with a total capacity of 1,200 seats.

Cathedral Square is a popular meeting place in Århus; it is often the site for open-air exhibitions of art, photographs and the like.

Immediately across from the theater, and dominating its surroundings, is the **cathedral**, with its rather odd collection of spires (see page 220). Directly behind this, on Domkirkeplads, is the complex that houses the **Women's Museum** and the rather unusual **Occupation Museum** (see pages 223 and 224).

As you continue, the street – now called **Mejlgade** – offers many contrasts. The lively mix of architectural styles is punctuated by a number of cafés, restaurants and boutiques. At number 19, on the left, a red timber-framed structure is now home to Jouls, a hardware shop. As the street narrows somewhat, the buildings become a little older; take some time to investigate the little alleyway at number 53, again on the left, that leads to the **Musik Caféen**. Mejlgade ends when it meets the much larger, and busier, **Nørreport**; here, at the left hand corner, is a store selling fashionable secondhand art-deco clothes and accessories that is highly popular with students at the nearby university. Secondhand Rose would probably find some bargains here.

Nørreport leads up a fairly steep incline toward the **Fine Arts Museum** (*Århus Kunstmusem*); this is at the tip of the **Vennelyst Park** (*Vennelystparken*), which was an amusement park in the 1800s. Today it forms part of the University Park, created in the 1930s to provide a pleasant setting for the institution.

Although undoubtedly light and modern, the somewhat bland and uninspiring architectural style of the museum buildings stands in stark contrast to the classical old apartment buildings across the road. The same can be said for the **Steno Museum** (*Stenomuseet*), located in C.F. Mollers Alle just off Høegh Guldbergs Gade at the top of the hill.

The quickest way to return to the center of town from here is to cross Høegh Guldbergs Gade into Fynsgade, then make a left onto Sjællandsgade and follow it down the hill; the street narrows somewhat towards the bottom as it meets Nørregade. From there, a quick right followed by a left onto Paradisgade brings you to **Studsgade**. Make a small detour left along Studsgade where, directly across from a modern furniture design store, are three diminutive but unusually brightly painted old wood-framed houses at numbers 36, 34 and 32.

The Latin Quarter

Retrace your steps to Studsgade, which soon leads into **Volden**. This area, with its narrow streets and a cosmopolitan ambiance of specialty stores, boutiques, secondhand bookshops, restaurants and bars is known as the Latin Quarter.

Halfway along, at Rosensgade, Volden opens into a small square dominated by a modernistic statue named *Madam*, which depicts a woman holding a baby. On the other side of this square is **Badstuegade**, which – along with Volden – ends at a pedestrian walkway called **Lille Torv** (easily recognizable by the 7-Eleven store, an incongruous landmark). Lille Torv, in turn, leads into **Store Torv**, which takes you back to the cathedral square.

To continue your tour, follow Vestergade away from Lille Torv; this takes you toward one of the oldest sights in Århus, the **Church of Our Lady** (*Vor Frue Kirke*) at Frue Kirkeplads (see page 221).

Århus Canal

Next, wind behind the Magasin du Nord department store, through a bland area made better only by the ochre and black timber-framed building that houses the Baghuset housing goods store. Walk through the arch and take the left turn that leads to the steps of the canal at Åboulevarden.

During the summer months, the canal area is the most popular meeting place in Århus. Its banks are lined with a plethora of restaurants and bars – including the ubiquitous Irish pubs. This area is also the heart of the shopping district in Århus, as is **Skt. Clemens Stræde**, a typically tiny pedestrian-only street around the corner.

The Ancient Town

The basement of the Unibank holds unexpected treasures.

At the end of Skt. Clemens Torv, at number 6, is a large branch of **Unibank**; in its basement you will find the unusual exhibits that constitute the **Viking Museum** (*Vikingemuseet*). Large-scale archaeological excavations on the site during 1963 and 1964 uncovered evidence of the original Viking settlement. Exhibits here are comprised of both original objects that were discovered and reproductions of the same. Access to the site is through the main entrance of the bank. Admission is free, but only during banking hours: Monday to Friday from 9:30 am to 4 pm; to 6 pm on Thursday.

To conclude the walking tour, follow **Skt. Clemens Torv**, **Søndergade** and **Ryesgade**; turn right into Sønder Allé, take the first left into Park Allé and you will be back at City Hall.

STRØGET AGAIN

Århus will soon have its own version of Copenhagen's Strøget. This will be a continuous shopping street, leading from Cathedral Square all the way to the railway station behind Rådhuspladsen, along Skt. Clemens Torv, Søndergade and Ryesgade.

A Stroll Through History

Århus

THE NATIONAL OPEN AIR MUSEUM OF URBAN HISTORY AND CULTURE
(*Den Gamle By*)
Viborgvej 2
☎ 86-12-31-88
www.dengamleby.dk

Outdoor museums are quite common in Scandinavia; the ones in Stockholm (at Skansen) and in Bergen come immediately to mind. Den Gamle By is considered to be Europe's largest, most comprehensive and most detailed. Under no circumstances should visitors to Århus fail to visit.

The very charming private grounds are enhanced by a lake populated with geese and ducks. You will find an eclectic collection of 75 historical houses, ranging

Take time out during your visit to Den Gamle By for refreshments at the Simonsens Have tea garden, and then take a horse and carriage ride through the grounds.

Be sure to bring some modern currency to Den Gamle By, in the event you have the opportunity to do some old-fashioned shopping.

from the Renaissance period to World War I, that have been moved here from locations all over Denmark. From the expansive merchants' homes to the smaller, more modest artisans' residences, interiors, for the most part, are historically intact. Giving the museum a further air of authenticity, the staff is in costume, and, at certain times of year, an old-fashioned baker's shop, bookshop and florist are open for business.

Exhibits include silverware, textiles and furnishings; Denmark's grandest toy museum; and the Danish Museum of Clocks and Watches. This is a highly interesting and informative museum, with collections spanning many cultural periods and encompassing their various economic strata.

Den Gamle By is reached by taking a number 3 bus from Århus' City Hall. Daily opening hours are January from 11 am to 3 pm; February, March, November and December from 10 am to 4 pm; April, May, September and October from 10 am to 5 pm; and June to August from 9 am to 6 pm. Admission during January, February and March is DKK 45; the rest of the year it is DKK 60.

Churches

CATHEDRAL
(*Århus Domkirke*)
☎ 86-12-38-45 or www.Århus-domkirke.dk

Measuring 93 m (305 ft) long, and equally high, this is the largest cathedral in Denmark; it is capable of holding 1,200 people.

The distinctive red brick Gothic façade seen today dates from the late 15th to early 16th centuries. Its history begins much farther back, however, in the 13th century. Bishop Peder Vognsen oversaw the construction of a Romanesque church on this site, which was dedicated to St. Clement, patron saint of sailors. Its walls were, at one time, covered by numerous decorative paintings but, as often happened, many disappeared during the Reformation. Nevertheless, this cathedral is still recognized as having retained more such paintings than any other church in Denmark. Most are from the end of the 15th and beginning of the 16th century; one, dating from around 1300, is not only the oldest piece of art in the cathedral but is the only one remaining from the original Romanesque structure.

Other notable pieces are the Renaissance-era carved oak pulpit; the font, cast in 1481; six fine wrought-iron latticework portals; and a single stained glass window that was installed in 1926. Undoubtedly, though, pride of place belongs to the principal altarpiece; it was inaugurated at Easter services in 1479. There is also a huge hanging **votive ship** dating from 1720. It is notable for being the largest in Denmark, and has a fascinating history.

Art lovers certainly will want to set aside ample time for investigating the cathedral's treasures.

The cathedral is open from January 1 to April 30, Monday through Saturday, 10 am to 3 pm; from May 1 to September 30, Monday through Saturday, 9:30 am to 4 pm; and between October 1 and December 31, Monday through Saturday, 10 am to 3 pm. Admission is free.

CHURCH OF OUR LADY
(*Vor Frue Kirke*)
Frue Kirkeplads
☎ 86-12-12-43 or www.aarhusvorfrue.dk

One of the oldest places in Århus, this church offers a complex of attractions – the great central nave, the chapel in the crypt, and the Abbey church – all set within lovely gardens that are decorated with statues and flagstones. The oldest parts of the church building itself date back to the middle of the 13th century. At that time, the site was handed over to the Dominicans, who constructed an abbey here; the church formed its southern building. What you see today is the result of extensive renovations in the 1950s, during which the amazing chapel in the crypt

Århus

was rediscovered. Built in 1060, the crypt is the oldest ecclesiastical building in Århus, as well as being the oldest arched space in Scandinavia.

The church was reconsecrated on November 10th, 1957, and now is in use again. It is open Monday to Friday from 10 am to 2 pm; and Saturday from 10 am to midday.

Museums

FINE ARTS MUSEUM
(*Århus Kunstmusem*)
Høegh Guldbergs Gade 2
☎ 86-13-52-55 or www.aarhuskunstmuseum.dk

The Århus Kunstmusem dates from 1859; it has the oldest art collection in Denmark outside of Copenhagen.

Exhibits include over 1,000 paintings, 300 sculptures and 11,000 paper-based forms of art. Look also for the best of Danish art from the mid-18th century to date, representing the Danish Golden Age, Romanticism, Realism and Impressionism.

The Kunstmuseum is open Tuesday to Sunday from 10 am to 5 pm; until 8 pm on Wednesday. Admission is DKK 40. The opening of a new modernistic cube-shaped brick building, to be located next to the Musikhuset and the Scandinavian Center, has been planned to coincide with the **Århus Festival Week** in August of 2003. Tourist Århus, ☎ 45-89-40-67-00, www.aarhusfestuge.dk.

STENO MUSEUM
(*Stenomuseet*)
C.F. Mollers Alle
☎ 89-42-39-75 or www.stenomuseet.dk

This is the Danish Museum for the History of Science and Medicine. Its exhibits are divided into two sections. The first explores the history of science from Stonehenge to Niels Bohr – with huge telescopes being particularly fascinating. The second details the history of medicine – with some intriguing life-size models and ancient equipment. The upper floor contains a planetarium.

A recent addition to this museum is the Medicinal Herb Garden, a quiet place in which to meditate or recuperate.

The Steno Museum is open Tuesday to Sunday from 10 am to 4 pm; and Wednesday evening from 7 pm to 10 pm. Planetarium shows are daily, at 11 am, 1 pm, 2 pm and 8 pm. Admission to the museum is DKK 40; an extra admission of DKK 40 is charged for Planetarium shows, but a combination ticket for the two, at DKK 60, offers a little savings.

WOMEN'S MUSEUM
(*Kvindemuseet*)
Domkirkplads 5
☎ 86-13-61-44 or wwwkvindemuseet.dk

The Women's Museum is a national specialist museum, opened to the public in 1984. Its stated aim is to collect exhibits and knowledge that will illustrate and preserve the changes, for better or worse, affecting women. It is directly across from the cathedral in an interesting old building, which was constructed as the Town Hall in 1857, and which served as a police station between 1941 and 1984.

You've come a long way, baby.

Between 1992 and 1994 the city of Århus completely renovated the building; it has been listed as a historical building since 1996. The renovation included the installation of the **Mathilde Fibiger Garden** as a small public square next to the museum. In addition to the permanent exhibits, three or four temporary exhibitions on aspects of women's history or art are featured annually.

The Women's Museum is open between January 1 and May 31, and between September 1 and December 31, Tuesday to Sunday from 10 am to 4 pm; between June 1 and August 31 it is open daily from 10 am to 5 pm. Admission is DKK 25.

By way of clarification, the name of this museum refers to wartime occupation – not to types of work.

OCCUPATION MUSEUM
(*Besættelsesmuseet*)
Mathilde Fibigers Have 2
☎ 86 18 42 77

The Besættelsesmuseet is in the same complex as the Women's Museum; exhibits are dedicated to all aspects of life during the period of German occupation, between 1940 and 1945. Ironically – or appropriately – these are housed in the cellars that were used by the Gestapo as headquarters from 1944 to 1945.

Unfortunately, the visiting hours are limited; the museum is open on Saturday and Sunday, throughout the year, from 11 am to 4 pm; from June to August it is also open on Tuesday and Thursday, during the same hours. Admission is DKK 20.

Shop Till You Drop

IMERCO
Søndergade 43
☎ 86-2-49-00

A member of the largest retail group in Denmark, this is the place to go for all aspects of Danish design for the home. Here you will find the most eclectic collection of housewares you ever are likely to see: kitchen utensils, bar equipment from Stelton of Denmark, crystal and glassware, china, flatware, clocks, and bathroom supplies. Pay attention, also, to the innovative weather stations designed by Jacob Jensen. Be sure to visit the second-floor art gallery.

EDITOR

Sønder Allé 5

☎ 86-12-77-20

Editor is, along with the bakeries, among the earliest opening stores in Århus.

For some reason, Denmark seems to have more than its share of shops specializing in pens, and this one stands above the rest of that genre in Århus.

Editor was founded, in 1946 by the present proprietor's father, who still arrives to open the store at 8 am every day. It certainly is a very traditional place, and offers a choice of the best brands in the business. Some are, to say the least, quite expensive. Apparently, the top-of-the-range Mont Blanc pen sells for close to DKK 2 million! Editor also has a wide range of calculators, automatic calendars and things of that ilk.

HELLY HANSEN SHOPPEN

Storetorv 7

☎ 86 12 13 21

This store, selling outerwear for the whole family, is a branch of the store of the same name in Copenhagen (see page 91).

GLASPUSTEREIT BÜLOW DUUS

Studsgade 14

☎ fax 86-12-72-86

Located in an attractive house in the city center, this will tempt you to take a break on your stroll through Århus. Not only will you be able to watch the fascinating process of glass blowing at the hands (and mouths) of real artisans, but you can also purchase these unique creations that range from drinking glasses, candlesticks, and bowls, to other more unusual items. Open Monday to Thursday from 9:30 am to 5:30 pm; Friday from 9:30 am to 7 pm; and Saturday from 10 am to 2 pm.

Go to Glaspustereit Bülow Duus to watch or to buy.

Århus

After Dark

ROYAL SCANDINAVIAN CASINO
Hotel Royal
Store Torv 4
☎ 86-12-00-11, fax 86-76-04-04

The elegant décor of the casino reflects the ambiance of the hotel. Its walls are covered with paintings by international artists. It is also divided into the classic casino, where you will find the table games, and the electronic casino, where the gaming is electronic. The casino is open from 2 pm to 4 am; identification, such as a passport, is required, and the minimum age is 18. Admission is DKK 40. Dress code is formal in the classic casino and informal in the electronic casino.

Baccarat, Blackjack, four tables; American Roulette, five tables; French Roulette, one table; 35 slot machines.

Best Places To Stay

The following hotels are listed in order of their price, starting with the most expensive. The stars reflect the **HORESTA** rating system (see page 10).

HOTEL ROYAL ★★★★
Store Torv 4
☎ 86-12-00-11, fax 86-76-04-04
www.hotelroyal.dk
102 rooms

If you are looking for classical and luxurious accommodation in Århus, look no further than the Hotel Royal.

Located in the heart of town close to the cathedral, this hotel has a magnificent façade, which is matched by its interior. The hotel offers three categories of accommodations. Royal Standard rooms meet the hotel's requirements for size, amenities and comfort, and many have a quiet position overlooking the yard. Royal de Luxe rooms have additional features, and are decorated with original works of art; these rooms also have fax machines. In this category, you can select from large rooms overlooking the cathedral square or the pedestrian streets, or quiet two-room junior suites. At the highest level are the luxury suites; these are newly decorated and include original artworks. Royal de Luxe suites also have fax machines and other amenities. Doubles from DKK 1,545 to DKK 3,000.

RADISSON SAS SCANDINAVIA HOTEL ★★★★

Margrethepladsen 1
☎ 86-12-86-65, fax 86-12-86-75
www.radisson.com/Århusdk
234 rooms

Just a short walk across a park from the City Hall, this is a modern and very tasteful hotel. It is part of the Scandinavian Center, which also houses a Congress Hall, a Shopping Center and an Office Complex.

The rooms are pleasantly furnished and excellently equipped. They are decorated in a variety of styles, including Scandinavian, British, Chinese and Japanese. An exclusive Presidential Suite and classy Junior Suites are available. Doubles from DKK 1,650 to DKK 1,850.

HOTEL PHILIP

Åboulevarden 28
☎ 87-32-14-44, fax 86-12-69-55
www.hotelphilip.dk
Eight suites

The restaurant is the main feature at Hotel Philip.

Expect things to be done a little differently at this small, elegant hotel with a great location alongside the Aa Canal. Everything here revolves around the restaurant where, surprisingly, you also check in.

Århus

The hotel is a bit exclusive, having only eight suites. All are large, offer every modern facility, and have either a French or Italian ambiance. The two on the top floor are decorated in a particularly romantic style.

SCANDIC HOTEL PLAZA ★★★
Banegardsplads 14
☎ 87-32-01-00, fax 87-32-01-99
www.scandic-hotels.com
161 rooms

In the town center and just across from the train station, this hotel has nicely furnished, well-equipped rooms. Other amenities include the **Brazil** restaurant, a cocktail bar, a gym, sauna and Jacuzzi, a solarium, a billiard room, and a garage. Doubles range from DKK 1,495 to DKK 1,995.

HOTEL ATLANTIC ★★
Europlads 10-14
☎ 86-13-11-11, fax 86-13-23-43
www.nordiskhotelgruppe.dk
102 rooms

Come to the Hotel Atlantic for a room with a view. Located in an impressively modern building across the road from the bay, this hotel boasts lovely views of the city and out over the water. The pleasant rooms each have a small balcony. A restaurant occupies the 10th floor. Doubles range from DKK 1,195 to DKK 1,395.

Best Places To Eat

PRINS FERDINAND
Den Gamle By
Vibogvej, 2
☎ 86-12-52-05

This classical restaurant is in a charming building just outside Den Gamle By (see page 220). Expect contemporary Danish gastronomy with international influences, fine wines, and other interesting touches, such as exclusively imported chocolates from Ecuador, Grenada and Venezuela. Not inexpensive (dinner will be about DKK 550), but a fine dining experience.

RESTAURANT SCENARIO
Margrethepladsen 1
☎ 86-12-86-65

In the Radisson SAS Scandinavia Hotel, this restaurant is a delightful surprise both in its ambiance and in its cuisine. Although the menu is limited, the choices are succulent and innovative indeed. For example, salmon wrapped in an herb potato rosti is served with a side dish of tiny marinated mushrooms in a lettuce cup, topped with edible flowers imported from Israel. Special dietary needs are catered to in the Vegetarian and Low Fat menus, and Restaurant Scenario's Fast Menu guarantees you will be served within 10 minutes. About DKK 400.

ALBUFETO
Fiskergade 28
☎ 86-19-46-11

Albufeto is a taste of Portugal in downtown Århus.

Its location, in a rather plain side street very close to the city center, belies the lovely interior of this Portuguese-style restaurant. Expect, of course, traditional Portuguese cod dishes and delicious shellfish

Århus

and fish combinations, as well as lamb chops and veal for those with other tastes; dinner will be about DKK 300. The wine list is also heavily Portuguese and features, among other vintages, Vinho Verde and a fine selection of port wines.

BRYGGEREIT SCT. CLEMENS
Kannikegade 10-12
☎ 86-13-80-00

St. Clement's is the only pub in Århus with its own brewery.

St. Clement's Brewery is adjacent to the cathedral square. The interior, as is common in such places, is an open-plan design.

The menu is presented in the form of a newspaper; the dishes are varied, wholesome and tempting. Dinner here will be about DKK 300. Wash it down, naturally, with beer, unfiltered and additive-free, brewed in accordance with ancient traditions.

A HEREFORD BEEFSTOUW
Skolegade 5
☎ 86-13-53-25

This restaurant is on the other side of the cathedral square from St. Clement's Brewery. As is explained more fully in the Copenhagen chapter (see page 127), this is an extraordinary restaurant in its concept, style and cuisine – despite being part of a chain – and never fails to delight in every sense. DKK 350.

L'ESTRAGON
Klostergade 6
☎ 86 12 40 66

Salmon fans will be "wild" about L'Estragon.

This is a tiny, charming French bistro-style restaurant with an inviting ambiance. The menu may be small, but it is quite eclectic. You will find such delicacies as wild salmon – they claim to be the only restaurant in Denmark to serve it – wild deer, and mallard. Three courses range from DKK 255, and four courses from DKK 315.

EMMERYS
Guldsmedgade 24-26
☎ 86-13-04-00

Emmerys offers an interesting melding of the old and new, with an ecological twist. It is, at one and the same time, the oldest pastry restaurant in Århus, the newest tapas bar in town, and home of an ecological bakery. Located on an interesting shopping street between Vor Frue Kirke and Lille Torv, Emmerys has a casually elegant ambiance. Dinner is about DKK 300.

Feast on gourmet creations at breakfast time, lunchtime and/or dinnertime at Emmerys.

Århus Information

Emergencies

Ambulance, police & fire . . . . ☎ 112
Medical . . . . ☎ 86-20-10-22
On call from 4 pm to 8 am weekdays, and on weekends.
Dental . . . . ☎ 40-51-51-62
On call 8-9 pm, and wekkends 9-10 am.

Newsstand

Foreign newspapers are available at Århus **Stiftstidendes**, Banegårdspladsen 6, ☎ 86-12-22-43.

Pharmacy

Århus Løve Apotek, Store Torv 5 . . . . ☎ 86-12-00-22
Open 24 hours.

Århus

Police

Police Station, Ridderstræde 1 ...... ☎ 87-31-14-48
Open 24 hours.

Post Office

The **main post office** is in the Central Train Station, Banegårdspladsen 1A, ☎ 89-35-80-00. Monday-Friday, 9:30 am to 6 pm, Saturday 10 am to 1 pm.

Tourist Office

TOURIST ÅRHUS
City Hall (*Rådhuset*)
Park Alle at Rådhuspladsen
☎ 89-40-67-00, fax 86-12-95-90
www.visitaarhus.com, info@visitaarhus.com

The **Århus Pass** (*Århus Passet*) allows free bus transportation within the municipality of Århus, free admission to many of the city's attractions, and even free parking in the Skolebakken car park. It's a smart way to stretch your traveling budget. The pass can be purchased at the tourist office, as well as at many hotels and a variety of other places. The cost for a one-day pass is DKK 88; a two-day pass is DKK 110; and a one-week pass is DKK 155.

Tourist office hours vary seasonally. Opening time is generally 9:30 or 10 am. Closing time ranges from 1 pm (weekends) to 4:30, 5 or 6 pm (weekdays). The office is always closed on national holidays.

Ribe

The town of Ribe is in the western part of Denmark, on the narrowest section of the Jutland peninsula. This is the **North Sea** coast of Denmark, though Ribe is sheltered by a series of islands in the **Wadden Sea** (*Vadehavet*) between Esbjerg, to the north, and Germany, about 50 kilometers to the south.

A Brief History

Ribe is considered to be Denmark's oldest town, having its origins sometime around the year 700 when a market took root on the eastern banks of the *Ribe Å* (Ribe River), near the spot where Sct. Nicolaj Gade is today. This market played host several times a year to merchants, craftsmen, and shoppers who traveled from lands far away. Eventually, it evolved into a meeting place between the Viking-controlled north and Western Europe, and a community began to grow around the market site. Modern archeological evidence paints a picture of Viking Ribe as being populated by fairly sophisticated artisans who made items of, among other things, leather, glass and amber.

The Cathedral & The Market

The earliest documented mention of Ribe can be traced to around 860, when it was noted that Ansgar, known as the Apostle of the North, had obtained a portion of land from the Danish king; he also received permission to construct a church in the region. No proof exists, however, that this actually came to pass. It can only be confirmed that a bishop lived in Ribe, and by definition a cathedral existed here, from 948, though the precise location of that cathedral has not been ascertained.

Ribe

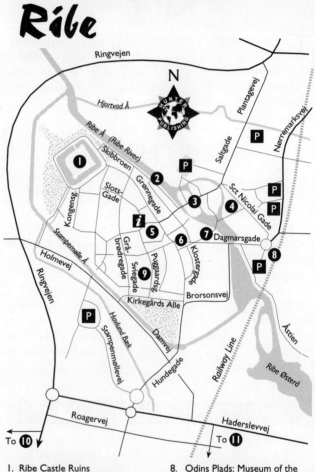

1. Ribe Castle Ruins
2. Flood Column; Fiskergade
3. Pedestrian Causeway
4. Ribe Art Museum & Garden
5. Torvet; Ribe Cathedral & Museum
6. Von Stockens Plads: Toy Museum; Old Town Hall
7. Sct. Catharinæ Plads: St. Catharinæ Church & Abbey

8. Odins Plads: Museum of the Viking Period; Train Station
9. Cathedral School
10. Wadden Sea Center; Mandø Island
11. Ribe Viking Center

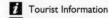 Tourist Information

 Parking

© 2003 HUNTER PUBLISHING, INC.

NOT TO SCALE

The 12th century was a time of rapid development in Ribe. First, the town expanded to encompass both sides of the river. In the latter part of that century, construction of the new, and present-day, cathedral began in the town center. This led to the establishment of more parish churches and abbeys, and of the fortifications necessary to defend them. Subsequently, Ribe cashed in on its trading potential, mainly exporting agricultural produce and importing and reselling clothing and luxury goods. In fact, it did so well for itself that it became the major Danish port on the North Sea and, also, the country's primary entryway into Western Europe by way of sea trade routes that linked it to England, Germany and the countries of the Mediterranean.

Wars & Floods

A series of tragedies hit Ribe dramatically, beginning in 1580 when it was devastated by a great fire. Less than a century later, its economic stability and influence as a major trading city were weakened by the sanding up of the river and by the emergence of new trade routes that vied for international business. Further exacerbating the problems were major floods that, as evidenced by records marked on Ribe's "flood column," reached as high as 19 feet above the normal water level in 1634. Wars with Sweden and an outbreak of the plague also took their toll in both lives and prosperity. Ironically, these circumstances, in combination with the blessing that no more major fires occurred after 1580, preserved the historic integrity of the city. The precipitous decline in the population meant there was little need for new construction, and the dire economic condition of those who remained left little in the way of funds for such endeavors. Therefore, many of the buildings that would, otherwise, have

Ribe

been rebuilt were not replaced; instead, people repaired what they already had.

Historic Preservation

The value of this architectural gem was finally recognized in 1899 when the Ribe Tourist Association beegan preserving these old houses, with the aim of making Ribe a major tourist attraction. In this they have succeeded. In the medieval town center, about 110 buildings have been restored. The entire area, composed of some 560 buildings, is the subject of a preservation order, a process to which the people who live there are enthusiastically dedicated. Visitors today will find Ribe to be a fascinating and charming throwback from the modern world, and no one can possibly leave disappointed.

Getting Here

By Train

From Copenhagen it is necessary to change to a southbound train to Ribe at **Bramming**, with the total journey taking about 3½ hours. ☎ 70-13-14-15, www.dsb.dk.

Getting Around

On Foot

Ribe's **Old Town** covers a small geographic area, and historic sites and restaurants are within an easy walk from the train station and hotels.

By Taxi

Taxis are available outside the main train station, or call ☎ 75-42-00-88.

Sunup To Sundown

A Stroll Around Ribe

Begin this walk at the Ribe tourist office at Torvet 3 (it is housed in a magnificent building named ***Porsborg***, which dates from 1590, adjacent to the Hotel Dagmar). From here, cross the street to the magnificently imposing **cathedral**.

Following the pedestrian walkway along the embankment, walk to the corner of Overdammen and Sortebrødreg. This is the home of the **Town Museum** (*Quedens Gaard*). However, this is now closed and it is not expected to reopen until 2005.

Turn left, and walk down Fiskergade; this street epitomizes the ancient charms of Ribe. To its left through narrow streets you get glances of Grønnegade, a reminder of the Dutch merchants from Groningen. On the other side of Fiskergade, small alleyways lead to the waterside street called **Skibbroen**. You will join this street at the bottom of Fiskergade. Skibbroen, a wider street, used to be the town wharf. These days it is a harbor for leisure craft and other boats. One of these is the ***Johanne Dan*** – one of the unusual flat-bottomed vessels that used to work the Wadden Sea. Half-timbered buildings line the street; some of these now house restaurants and bars.

As you walk, a strange, tall column is sure to draw curiosity. This is the **Flood Column** (*Stormflodssøjlen*). As can be seen from the countryside across the river this is very flat land and, as such, has always been susceptible to flooding. The rings around the column indicate the worst of these excesses. The highest floodline, commemorating the disaster of 1634, is over 6 m (19.7 ft) above the normal waterline.

If you look forward to shopping in Ribe, remember that stores close at 1 pm on Saturday, though they stay open until 3 pm on the first Saturday of the month.

Follow Skibbroen to the right until it rejoins Overdammen; this street, along with Mellendammen and Nederdammen, is the main **shopping area** of Ribe, and on sunny Saturday mornings these streets are colorful and busy indeed. Some of the buildings along the way are quite grand, but perhaps more interesting are the **mills** being turned by the fast-flowing waters that run in torrents under Mellendammen.

WHEN THE STORKS RETURN

If you are passing this way between late March and the end of August, make a particular point of looking toward the roof of the Town Hall for a view of the large nest that sits there; and therein lies a story. Storks, who spend the winter in Africa, quite like to live in Denmark in the summer months, and have been known to do so for over 500 years. In fact, the flat marshlands that surround Ribe are an ideal habitat for them, as it provides plentiful supplies of frogs and small fish, their cuisine of choice. The storks grace few towns, but Ribe is, and has been for many centuries, one of them.

Ribe is known throughout Denmark as "The town of the storks."

The storks follow the warm spring air currents across Europe, and usually arrive in late March, the males arriving first to ready the nest. In earlier times, there were many pairs; these days, however, just one pair arrives to make its summer home atop the Old Town Hall. They usually breed two or three chicks, who must be strong enough by the end of August to make the long flight back to Africa.

At the end of Nederdammen, a right turn onto Sct. Nicolai Gade will lead you to the **Ribe Art Museum** (*Ribe Kunstmuseum*) at number 10. Behind the museum, a pathway leads you to a charming detour away from the hustle and bustle. Initially, the path goes through the museum's magnificent **garden** and its famous **Turkish gazebo**; it then crosses a bridge over the river before passing back out to Sct. Catharinæ Plads. Turn left along the wider **Dagmarsgade**. This leads over another bridge, back across the river, to a traffic circle outside the railroad station. That, though, is not your destination. Instead, aim for the modern building on the left, which houses the **Museum of the Viking Period and Middle Ages** (*Ribes Vikinger*, see page 245).

The next stop on the walk is **Sct. Catharinæ Kirke** (St. Catharinæ's Church); it is clearly identified by its towering spire (see page 243). From **Odins Plads**, stroll back down along Dagmarsgade. Take a few moments on the bridge overlooking the river and enjoy the view of the meadows alongside it. If, by chance, you see some young lads fishing you might be surprised, and they might be too, by the size of their catch.

Just across Von Støckens Plads, at number 2, the **Toy Museum** (*Ribe Legetøjsmuseum*) is a modern structure that houses exhibits of a whimsical nature (see page 245).

Follow Sønderportsgade to **Puggaardsgade**. Although its history dates back to the beginning of the 13th century, many of the properties you see now originated in the 16th century. This is particularly obvious in the row of half-timbered houses near the junction with Sønderportsgade that were built around 1600. One of the most prominent, on the left side of the road, is **Taarnborg** a fascinating building constructed in the middle of the 16th century as the mansion of a nobleman. Later, from the mid-

Ribe

18th to the mid-19th century, it became the residence of Ribe's bishops.

A little farther ahead, and recessed to the right, is the **Cathedral School**. This building was given a major overhaul between 1977 and 1978, but actually dates from 1856 (it is thought that the first Cathedral School, most likely in premises closer to the cathedral itself, originated in 1145). **Gravsgade**, which intersects with Puggaardsgade, also has many fine examples of half-timbered and other old houses.

Turn right from Gravsgade into **Sviegade**, where the houses are tiny, with very low doorways. These are not quite so old or attractive as the ones we have just passed. Continue along, and follow Grabrødregade and then Grydergade, the latter more interesting than the former, back to Torvet to end the stroll.

Churches

At various times throughout the day, the carillon within the cathedral tower serenades those listening below with a combination of hymns and traditional folk tunes.

CHURCH OF OUR LADY
(*Domkirken*)
Torvet
☎ 75-42-06-19

The most impressive and dominant structure in Ribe – the Cathedral – is visible for miles around in the flat countryside surrounding the town.

It is known that a diocese was established at Ribe in AD 948. Earlier cathedrals, of wooden construction, are believed, but not confirmed, to have stood on this same site prior to the 12th century. Although work began on the present, Romanesque-style structure around the middle of the 12th century, another hundred years had passed before it finally was completed.

The cathedral was fashioned mainly of tufa-stone, along with some German sandstone and Jutlandic granite. Tufa-stone is a rock of volcanic origin found in the hills south of Cologne, Germany. This material had to be transported by ferryboat down the Rhine and then along the North Sea coastline to get to the construction site at Ribe.

The original design incorporated two towers of equal height on the cathedral's outer, west, wall. Disaster struck on Christmas Day in 1283, when one of these towers collapsed, killing many of the people worshiping inside. This tower was replaced, some 50 years later, by the square-shaped and formidable 52-m (170-ft) **Commoners' Tower** seen today. In 1594, a corner of this later tower also collapsed, causing a tall spire to come crashing down. This seeming instability in the structure is probably due to the fact that the cathedral is situated on a hill in swampy marshland; over time, the ground has sunk about 1.5 m (nearly 5 ft) below the street level. These days, a viewing platform at the top of the restored Commoners' Tower allows for a marvelous perspective of the town, out over the red roofs below, and impressive views of the surrounding countryside. Unfortunately, you will have to climb 248 steps to reach it.

Around the time that the Commoners' Tower was added, various other Gothic-style modifications were made. Among these was the addition of a row of chapels along each side, transforming the cathedral into a five-aisled church, the only one of its kind in all of Denmark.

The Reformation of 1536 brought with it the usual changes, although it wasn't until the very late 16th century that the Catholic altar was replaced with one in the Renaissance style.

Much of the interior decoration of the church during the Renaissance originated not by order of the church authorities themselves, but by private citizens anxious to have themselves, and their families, memorialized by engraved tombstones inside the ca-

Ribe

thedral. This was not an inexpensive proposition, and the less affluent sometimes resorted to using second-hand stones that they had smoothed over and re-carved with a new inscription. Upon close inspection, the old inscriptions are easily identifiable.

The series of natural and economic disasters that befell Ribe in the 17th century took their toll on the cathedral (the flood of 1634 actually reached all the way inside the cathedral to a level marked on a pillar behind the pulpit). For almost 200 years, no funds were available to effect the sorely needed repairs, and the building was left to fall into ruin.

It wasn't until the middle of the 19th century that the cathedral's importance as a national historical monument was recognized. Restoration work was initiated and carried out between 1882 and 1904. From this period of comprehensive restructuring and interior redecoration, the cathedral took on its present appearance.

Among the more important exterior changes was the addition of a massive bronze door, sculpted by **Anne Marie Carl-Nielsen**, on its southern side. The door incorporates a large, 13th century lion's head doorknocker, from whence comes the name the **Cat's Head** door. The head is surrounded by four saurians, lizard-like creatures that symbolize the strength of the Christian church amidst worldly chaos. As an interesting aside, locals relate a tradition that dictated the granting of asylum to anyone, including those accused of crimes, who was able to make their way to this lion's head.

RIBE CASTLE

The castle at Ribe is a ruin, but it is the site of a statue of Queen Dagmar; this is another example of the work of sculptor Anne Marie Carl-Nielsen, the wife of composer Carl Nielsen.

Looking up, you will find a massive, semi-circular sculpture in granite that is, in fact, the largest medieval sculpture in Denmark. This, *The Deposition from the Cross*, is a scene in The Heavenly Jerusalem wherein the crowds, including figures representing royalty, are depicted in the presence of Christ and the Virgin Mary.

The interior of the cathedral was totally restored and redecorated as well, although the choir stalls, the branched candelabrum and the font date from its medieval period. The most recent embellishments – a series of mosaics and frescos, new stained-glass windows, and a new communion table designed by Carl-Henning Pedersen – were added between 1982 and 1987.

Access to the church and tower is allowed only when services are not in progress, and hours vary seasonally and during holidays. Admission is DKK 12.

ST. CATHARINÆ CHURCH AND ABBEY
(*Sct. Catharinæ Kirke*)
Catharinæ Plads
☎ 75-42-05-34.

St. Catharinæ was originally founded in the early 13th century as an abbey for the Black Friars, as the Dominican order was known.

There were two earlier churches on this site before the present one was constructed in the 15th century. During the Reformation it was converted into a parish church and hospital, but by the early 20th century the structure had declined so badly that a novel way of reclaiming it was utilized – namely, using numerous jacks underneath it (one still survives) to bring it back to the perpendicular. One of the outstanding features of Skt. Catharinæ is the charming cloister.

Access to the church and abbey is only allowed when services are not in progress, and hours vary seasonally. From May to September, Sct. Catharinæ is open daily, 10 am to midday, and 2 to 5 pm. From October

Ribe

to April it closes at 4 pm. Admission is free for the church and DKK 3 for the Abbey.

The next stage of the walk takes you through quiet streets lined with numerous, and sometimes quite different structures. These are charming in their own right and stand at all kinds of funny angles. At the corner of Sønderportsgade and von Støckens Plads you will find the **Old Town Hall** (*Det Gamle Rådhus*), and the small museum known as **The Town Hall Collection** (see page 247).

Museums

RIBE ART MUSEUM
(*Ribe Kunstmuseum*)
Sct. Nicolai Gade 10
☎ 75-42-03-62, fax 75-42-21-82

The stately structure that houses the Ribe Art Museum was built by an affluent merchant between 1860 and 1864 in the Dutch Renaissance style. This national landmark building contains an interesting collection of Danish art dating from the mid-18th century.

The exhibits range from the time of the foundation of the Royal Danish Academy of Fine Arts in 1754 to the mid-20th century. Notable among these are paintings from the Danish Golden Age (1800-1850); the Naturalism and Realism period at the end of the 19th century; and even more modern examples of French impressionism.

Open daily, mid-June through August, 11 am to 5 pm; the rest of the year it is open Tuesday to Saturday, 1 pm to 4 pm; and Sunday, 11 am to 4 pm. Admission DKK 30.

MUSEUM OF THE VIKING PERIOD AND MIDDLE AGES
(*Ribes Vikinger*)
Odins Plads 1
☎ 75-88-11-22, fax 75-88-11-66
www.ribesvikinger.dk

A Viking marketplace existed along the banks of the river as long ago as AD 700. Excavations have discovered a treasure trove of archeological finds. These are now on display in a building that, until 1923, was Ribe's power station. Far from being mundane, this is a particularly innovative and interesting museum. In addition to the ancient Viking relics, there are full-size reconstructions of portions of the town, allowing visitors to see how Ribe appeared in the 9th and 15th centuries. The museum café should not be overlooked. It faces the river with the cathedral as a backdrop. The museum is open year-round, though days and hours vary seasonally. Admission DKK 50.

Discover more about the Viking Age through the Museum's multi-media experience, Wodan's Eye.

TOY MUSEUM
(*Ribe Legetøjsmuseum*)
Von Støckens Plads 2
☎ 75-41-14-40

This unique collection consists of thousands of toys dating from 1860 to 1980. Expect to find over 500 dolls, 600 cars, along with motorbikes, Danish fire engines and other rescue service vehicles, mechanical toys, and more. If you have old dolls for sale, or that need to be repaired, this is certainly the place to take them. The Toy Museum is open January, February, March, November and December, daily except Saturday, 1 pm to 4 pm; April, May, September and October, daily, 1 pm to 5 pm; and June, July and August, daily, 10 am to midday and 1 pm to 5 pm. Admission DKK 35.

Ribe

OLD TOWN HALL
(*Det Gamle Rådhus*)
Von Stockens Plads
☎ 76-88-11-22, fax 76-88-11-35

Ribe's Town Hall, a distinguished structure that dates from around the beginning of the 16th century, is the oldest in Denmark. It was originally built as a house of commerce. The building was converted later into a residential property; in 1619 it was the birthplace of the poet, Anders Bording, who published Denmark's first newspaper in Copenhagen in 1666. It changed uses again in the early 18th century, when town authorities bought it for use as the Town Hall; its present silhouette dates from restoration work done around 1900.

The section of the Town Hall that was once the debtors' prison now holds the **Town Hall Collection**. This is an exhibition of justice through the centuries and features, among other things, such gruesome items as executioner's swords, thumbscrews and spiked maces.

Open in May and September, Monday to Friday, 1 pm to 3 pm; and in June, July and August, daily, 1 pm to 3 pm. Admission to the collection is DKK 15.

After Dark

The Watchman's Rounds

Every night between May 1 and September 15, and on Fridays and Saturdays all year, the famous Ribe night watchman pays a visit to the Hotel Dagmar.

This offers a fascinating, first hand, way of learning about Ribe's historical importance. Not the least of the attractions is the Watchman himself. Dressed in a traditional uniform, wearing the monarch's initials engraved on a chain around his neck, and carrying an iron-spiked staff and a lamp, he strolls the cobblestone streets, regaling his followers with interesting historic anecdotes (told in the language of his audience) and his rendition of the special watch-man's song. Between May 1 and September 15, the Watchman departs each evening from **Weis Stue** at Torvet, 2, at around 10 pm. To accommodate the de-mand during the height of the tourist season, be-tween June 1 and August 21, and at a handful of other times throughout the year, an additional tour departs at 8 pm. Stop in at the Tourist Bureau (page 252) or www.ribetourist.dk for a brochure describing this and other guided tours.

Just Outside Ribe

There are three side-trips of interest, but they are all a little way outside of the town itself. The best way to visit them is by car or taxi.

Mandø Island

The community at *Mandø By* remains almost un-touched, and it is almost unreachable: at high tide, there is no route connecting it to the mainland. Dur-ing the summer months, and at other selected times, the only way to the island is at low tide, when a de-lightful open-topped bus pulled by a tractor takes you across the sands. Once there, you can rent a bike. There are also three walking trails, and bird-watching is good here. The bus to the island leaves from the car park to the west of the town of **Vester Vedsted**. For information about visiting Mandø, ☎/fax 75-44-51-07.

Wadden Sea Center

This nature center (*Vadehavscentret*) is on the main-land near the departure point for Mandø Island. A visit will teach you about life in and around the Wadden Sea. The center has nature and cultural ex-hibits, along with a multi-media show about storm

Ribe

surges – an ever-increasing threat in this area. Open April to September, 10 am to 5 pm, and October to March, 10 am to 4 pm; closed in January and December. Okholmvej 5, Vester Vedsted, DK-6760, Ribe; ☎ 75-44-61-51, fax 75-44-61-01, www.vadehavscentret.dk.

Ribe Viking Center

Each year, for two days in early May the Ribe Viking Center has the world's largest Viking Market.

Interest in the Scandinavian countries during the Viking times is, quite naturally, very high, and many towns have outdoor museums where the natives can learn about this aspect of their own history. Not to be outdone, Ribe has its own center where, in addition to exhibits detailing family life, a Viking Manor, and a reconstruction of Ribe town around 825, you can also take part in activities such as archery, traditional crafts and Viking games.

The Viking Center is open from May through September. Days and hours vary depending on the season, and hours are generally 11 am to 4 pm. Admission is DKK 50; guided tours by reservation are DKK 175 for a half-hour, or DKK 300 for one hour. The center is two kilometers (3.25 miles) south of Ribe. Lustrupvej 4, Lustrupholm, DK-6760, Ribe, ☎ 45-75-41-16-11, fax 45-75-41-16-20; www.ribevikinge-center.dk.

Best Places To Stay

HOTEL DAGMAR
Torvet
☎ 75-42-00-33, fax 75-42-36-52
www.hoteldagmar.dk
50 rooms

This hotel is in the historic center of Ribe. Dating from 1581, it holds the distinction of being the oldest hotel building in Denmark.

The current structure was first built as a mansion, however, replacing an earlier structure that had succumbed to the fire of 1580. Beginning just over a century later, around 1700, and continuing until 1800, it served as the residence for Ribe's Grand Mayors. At the end of this period, it donned a new hat – that of manor house inn – receiving its present name in 1912, following a major renovation. These days it boasts 50 pleasant and well-appointed double rooms and a charming ambiance.

The Hotel Dagmar has an on-site gourmet restaurant, as well as the less formal Watchman's Cellar bar/restaurant and an outdoor café that opens onto the old town square. DKK 1,025-DKK 1,375; extra bed for one to two children, DKK 125; rates include breakfast.

DEN GAMLE ARREST ★★
Torvet 11
☎ 75-42-37-00, fax 75-42-37-22, e-mail dga2505@post-14.tele.dk

Situated right alongside the cathedral, this was originally the curate's residence. Later it was used as a girl's school. Then, from 1893 to 1989, it served time, as the name implies, as the **Old Jail**. Beginning in 1992 its sentence was commuted and its ensuing transformation saw the old cells creatively converted into simply furnished rooms. A pleasant restaurant and a tasteful boutique that occupies the former guards' room round out the package. Double with shared bath, DKK 540-690; with private bath, 790-890. Rates include breakfast. DKK 25 extra per person, per night in July and August.

Ribe

Best Places To Eat

HOTEL DAGMAR
Torvet
☎ 75-42-00-33

This is, undoubtedly, *the* place to eat in Ribe. In a setting of considerable charm and gracious ambiance, diners cannot help but appreciate a menu composed and prepared each day, using only the freshest of ingredients. These are carefully selected by the chef himself on daily visits to the fish and vegetable markets. Selections may be made from a fixed-price menu, with a choice of three starters, three main courses and three desserts; or from the à la carte menu, which, on any given evening, may offer such tempting choices as air-dried graylag goose with mushroom stew, marshland lamb with baked garlic and basil sauce, and any number of tasty fish dishes. Alternatively, opt for the "Dagmar Dinner" of either two or three courses.

WEIS STUE
Torvet, 2
☎ 75-42-07-00

This restaurant is in a distinguished, albeit rather wobbly looking, half-timbered frame building that houses one of Denmark's oldest inns. The interior, which dates from around 1704, is notable for its decorated, beamed ceiling, wooden paneling and Dutch tiles. The restaurant has a limited menu with an emphasis on beef, veal and pork dishes offered at reasonable prices.

Ribe Information

Emergencies

Ambulance, police & fire . . . . ☎ 112
Medical . . . . ☎ 75-15-88-08
Information is also available at the Tourist Office.

Library

Giortz Plads . . . . ☎ 75-42-17-00
Internet access and local historical archives.

Newsstand

Kiosk Centrum, Torvet 13 . . . . ☎ 75-42-00-83

Pharmacy

Ribe Apotek, Tvedgade 19A . . . . ☎ 75-42-07-55

Police

Main station, Tangevej 4A . . . . ☎ 75-42-06-44

Post Office

Main branch, Sct. Nicolai Gade 12 . . . . ☎ 79-12-12-12

Tourist Office

RIBE TOURIST OFFICE
Torvet 3, DK-6760 Ribe
☎ 75-42-15-00, fax 75-42-40-78
www.ribetourist.dk, infotur@ribekom.dk

The tourist office is housed in a magnificent building named *Porsborg*, adjacent to the Hotel Dagmar. In addition to the expected tourist information and a

Ribe

range of souvenirs, it offers a booking service for travel and accommodations, and, outside of regular banking hours, it will (for a nominal fee) change small amounts of cash. Hours vary seasonally, with opening times generally around 9 or 10 am and closing around 4:30 or 5 pm.

Index